Asking

Shawna Lemay

Asking

Shawna Lemay

Seraphim
EDITIONS

The publisher gratefully acknowledges the financial assistance of the Canada
Council for the Arts.

Canada Council   Conseil des arts
for the Arts   du Canada

Library and Archives Canada Cataloguing in Publication

Lemay, Shawna, 1966-, author
      Asking / Shawna Lemay.

Poems and poem-essays.
ISBN 978-1-927079-27-0 (pbk.)

      I. Title.

PS8573.E5358A85 2014   C811'.54   C2014-901140-7

Editor: Robert Priest
Design and Typography: Rolf Busch
Author Photo: Robert Lemay
Cover Art: Robert Lemay - Garden Rose, 48" x 40" oil on canvas

Published in 2014 by
Seraphim Editions
54 Bay Street
Woodstock, ON
Canada N4S 3K9

Printed and bound in Canada

CONTENTS

CONVERSATIONS

GESTURES

One day I'm going to write a screenplay for a movie and the whole thing is just going to be people gesturing and talking and sometimes murmuring and breathing a certain way in front of paintings at a museum. I'm not sure yet just which paintings. Nothing too famous, but with just the correct verging toward obscurity.

Part of the screenplay will describe the way people whoosh by a painting. The sound they make. Maybe the person has already seen it, sat with it for half an hour, and walking by they don't want to look, don't want to spoil the time they had with it. Or they swooooosh, swish and swirl by, because they don't know the painting, or it doesn't speak to them at present. Or they are going to fly by, but something stops them, they're arrested mid-flight. The sound of shoes on a hardwood or cement floor. Scuffs, shuffling, clacking. Glissade, frappé, fondu, pirouette.

It's about space and about intervals, a stance. Dust motes. About patience and about looking at looking. It's about a ballet of small gestures. Hands on the hip, behind the back, flipping of hair, pointing, and then sliding of hands and arms into clumsy arabesques. Mainly this thing is about hands inhabiting a colour drunk space.

The tender light that surrounds a person looking at a painting, absorbed and at times reverent, at other times bored and uninterested and possibly even agitated.

One section of the screenplay will be devoted to Stendhal Syndrome. Sometimes called Florence Syndrome or hyperkulturemia. "As I emerged from the porch of Santa Croce, I was seized with a fierce palpitation of the heart; the wellspring of life was dried up within me, and I walked in constant fear of falling to the ground." This was Stendhal, 1817. Dizzyness, confusion, faintness, shortness of breath, heart palpitations characterize the condition.

The video footage of Jackson Pollock dripping paint onto a canvas always makes me feel like moving my arms. If you just concentrate on his arms you might start to think of birds, wingspans, gliding, hunting, drifting.

For some this is close to prayer. You can see that others are cold to the experience of standing in front of a painting, though. But when you place an artwork in a museum, it changes it, elevates it. Some people have headphones on, and walk around as if in fog, murky and slow. Feeling their way forward, they walk robotically, mechanically. They put their hands on their chins.

I've cried in front of paintings before. The Vermeer, *Study of a Young Woman*, in the Metropolitan Museum of art, for example. I keep telling people about it and I wrote about it once on my blog, which is bad because the more I try to explain it, the further away from the experience I seem to get. The thing is the huge sobs that came out of me, what were they? So unexpected. It escaped me and still escapes me. I left myself. An entire existence may be encompassed by an unexpected and wild sob from the depths.

More recently we went to Amsterdam and The Hague. Saw *Girl with the Pearl Earring* at The Mauritshuis. I'd seen it reproduced so many times, I assumed I'd be a bit numb to it in person. Not at all, not at all. Okay, maybe this sounds dumb, but here is the best way I can think to describe it - that light entered my heart. Also, a *lightness*, but more like a sharp and real shard of buttery light. And so if there's an ache in my chest right now, I'll ascribe it to that precise moment when I so desperately wanted to feel something beautiful, as beautiful as love and other annunciations, and that I did.

And it makes me smile now to think my experience was this poetic and divine submission to the earthly glow, the inner fire and silence of the painting, where I melted right into it, an honored guest, felt myself looking over my shoulder and pierced by the pearl earring I would later buy a replica pair of in the museum gift shop.

A long time ago, when I first started seeing Rob a friend said to me, he gets *that* much money for a *stupid* painting? She packed a lot of venom in that word *stupid*, and it's stuck with me ever since.

Twenty years after the word stupid, we're still struggling to make ends meet, to pay the bills. But I think we live elegantly enough. We try.

There's an area around a painting hung in a museum that's filled with the telepathic juice and butter of its haunting. Dreams pour out of some paintings, frothy and delectable, fierce palpitations. For what it's worth, part of my screenplay will be about the absence of people and gestures, what the space looks like when someone has just left it, when the guard is off in the corner waiting or dozing or checking their email or looking at it out of the corner of an eye. How the space is soaked and iridescent and utterly defocused and unresolved so that one must swim back into it, pulled into a current, arms flailing but gently without fear of falling into its cool and starry depths.

SWOON

I thought by now I'd have logged more time with the women who come and go talking of Michelangelo. Or Anselm Kiefer or Judy Chicago or Paula Modersohn-Becker. In my twenties I went to university because I imagined I'd have long conversations about the nature of art, of beauty. That just going to university would be the beginning of this conversation. And it was, only mostly I have it with myself.

Who has time to think about beauty, or read essays by Susan Sontag where she quotes Gertrude Stein who said that to call a work of art beautiful means that it is dead. Is beauty dead? Are we deadened? Do we believe in art? How that question is tied to the one, do we believe in beauty? Well, we might not, we might not believe in or be consoled by delicate and breakable old beauty, but Sontag says that: "the capacity to be overwhelmed by the beautiful is astonishingly sturdy and survives amidst the harshest distractions." We can experience beauty, even if it is sometimes tough to believe in. I believe we can still be astonished by beauty and apples, if not by Vogue magazine and the way 14 year old girls are used to advertise products targeted at 45 year old women.

If you study art or write poetry it's impossible to avoid the subject of beauty, or at least it should be IMHO. You might ramble through the history of beauty, of aesthetics. Hit upon Kant, Nietzsche, Sartre, read the lines by Keats, "Beauty is truth, truth beauty , – that is all. / Ye know on earth, and all ye need to know." This is just the tip of the philosophy of beauty iceberg of course, and you can't think about beauty without bringing in ideas of the sublime, or wrestle with the notion of ugliness.

It's become unfashionable to talk about beauty, beauty has become neglected, you read this from time to time. It's problematic, it's suspect. And it is, you know it is. But people are still arguing for it, quietly, persistently. Kinds of beauty, rather than Beauty. Which itself is pretty beautiful.

What do we talk about when we talk about beauty? (That's a bit of a rip-off of a Raymond Carver title which you probably knew but in case you didn't. It's impossible to catch every single allusion right?). I like to talk about how it's never one thing, that there are so many possible permutations and that it's always shifting, our idea of what might be beautiful. The hairstyles and shoes of the 18th century compared to the ones in the 21st century. Discuss.

I make it a point to read or make or attempt to write something beautiful every day. So much failure.

You might say failure has a side to it that's quite beautiful and light-filled. There's the potential for light, sidelight, in these instances.

Maybe I'm more interested in light these days than beauty. The way it eases through the slats in a fence late in the day, so golden and sneaky and surprising.

I'm interested in being overwhelmed by beauty, the sturdy experience of it. I'm interested in the swoon. That thing that happens before something overwhelming. A sort of brain-swoon, like brain freeze, the thing you get when you quickly drink a slushy drink from the corner chain store. You've mixed it just the way you like, lime, cream soda and coke with a touch of Mountain Dew on top. A kind of ugly sluiced rainbow. Which has nothing to do with the sensation – the sensation that you expect but doubt.

What about the people who drive to their jobs in office towers or warehouses or windowless shopping malls? I guess I've been one of those people often enough. So let me tell you it's quite possible that the expectation or hope of brain-swoon melts away from you. And it hurts, throbs, if you've known beauty however thinly, however splintered.

Listen. If I have known beauty
let's say I came to it
asking

(That's Phyllis Webb)

I've learned to stay away from women who come and go and refuse to talk about Michelangelo. Of course with the friends I have, we talk about our children as well, about what and who we love, and sometimes we exchange recipes and gossip and tell stories. But there's this one person I keep meeting, Hélène Cixous talks about this phenomena, of meeting the same person in a different guise throughout a life, the one who impedes us from living joy. Living the blue flower. Or reaching for the blue flower. The blue and delicate longing that lies incessantly at one's heart.

"I have no craving to be rich, but I long to see the blue flower. It lies incessantly at my heart and I can imagine and think of nothing else. Never did I feel like this before. It is as if until now I had been dreaming, or as if sleep had carried me into another world. For in the world I used to live in, who would have troubled himself about flowers?"

(This is from the novel *The Blue Flower* by Penelope Fitzgerald about the German poet and philosopher Novalis)

In Buddhism, there is also the recognition of the soul who repeats in your life, for a reason. Which has to do with what you can learn from that person, how to be kinder, better. Remember the rules that Henry James set out: "Three things in human life are important: the first is to be kind; the second is to be kind; and the third is to be kind." Or maybe in repeated meetings, encounters, what happens is that you learn how to relate to this person who perhaps works in the cubicle next to you every single livelong day so that you can smile like the Dalai Llama. You learn how to smile and wave, smile and wave, and how to be in their presence, at peace with yourself and you find out how at last, you can simply take a few steps back, and then walk away, smiling.

There is the beauty of thanking one's enemies. There were two bully girls, we called them the mean girls, where I once worked, years ago now. I tried many approaches with them. But in the end I read somewhere that sometimes the only way to resolve such dreadful blue flower killing episodes is with your feet. So I left. And it took me a while to find beauty again, but you know it was always there. It took years but now I thank them, even though for a while I felt like the next best thing to unemployable, because of the paths I've been on since. Without their insidious and secret meanness who knows where I'd be.

A terrible thought got me through this ordeal with the mean girls though. I didn't think they knew how to experience beauty, and I did. Rotten, I know, and possibly wrong. For them, I imagined a murky rainbow brain freeze rather than brain swoon. Still do. Can't help it.

Be happy and write. That's a line from an Ondaatje poem. I always think of the line in fancy curly brackets, but I don't think it's printed this way.

{Be happy and write}. It's sort of a happy/beautiful line though because it's so futile. Even so it's bored into me. Someone is telling this to the narrator who is going through a kind of personal hell, fleeting though it is, he has no way of seeing his way out at present. The narrator responds, not happy, but lucky, yes.

When I'm writing I'm usually happy, but kind of a weird tortured perfectly grey happy you know. A delicate heartbreaking tenuous happy. An overcast happy but with that soft light on a light blue wall. Rilke (who Ondaatje references in his poem) says, "I basically do not believe that it matters to be happy in the sense in which people expect to be happy." I have this underlined in my copy in a very vibrant spring green colour. May green.

Rilke, this mournful castle dwelling creature has a lot to say about working cheerfully, about how magnificent this unforeseeable life of ours is, how to endure, how to get through. His was a gloomy happiness, and what beauty he produced! Impossible to argue with that at least it is for me.

The passionate flying of strange birds and terrifying angels. That's as good a plagiarized definition of beauty as any perhaps.

The rejection of beauty troubles me. How people hold themselves quite intentionally from the experience of beauty. A withholding of the self. I guess I've made peace with the rejection of things that I've created, things I've tried to fill with light so that they might be of interest. I'm interested in strange little bits myself, things not for everyone. Beauty for mad women, that kind of beauty. The kind of beauty that refuses to be called dead. I'm interested yes in going on, working toward it anyway.

EXPRESSO

I'm going to imagine a line of poetry that's a single colour, a single mark: that juicy and confident.

The mark is lonely, the artist at the height of her powers. It's a tendril of light.

Imagine a painter who has been working for upwards of twenty years. Steadily. The mark might be made in the dead of some tender night, in complete darkness, eyes closed. This is the sort of thing I think about when I have insomnia. I close my eyes and make marks.

I imagine when I wake up there will be this colour, a gesture, which helps me go back to sleep, or maybe it's what's keeping me up – hard to say. It could be the light side of an apricot, an apricot in the light that happens slowly after a rain shower. An easing. A sort of apology. Or atonement is a more interesting word in this context so let's use that.

Intuitive, deliberate, confident. A bit mysterious, casual, sensual, even yes violent, blazing, but controlled. It's like a touch on your shoulder, like turning a page in a novel late at night quiet so you don't wake anyone. What I'm saying is that you're alone, but then not, you feel someone you love walking by, they touch you.

It's also timeless, glamorous, dappled, and full of luck. The line says, lucky, lucky, lucky you.

It's gravy, it's blood, it's nail polish. It glides, full of grace. It's full. It's empty. Clean. Freighted.

I don't think it's theoretical, but it holds up, it holds up, it has a trellis, this tendril does. It flakes, absorbs, it's pouring itself, buttery and syrupy. Or the line is just a smudge of jam on the book you were reading over breakfast.

When you dream about a long clothes line, the clothes have dried and smell like summer, and you know that butterflies have lit upon them and moved off, when you dream of reeling it in, there's no sound. No horrible squeaking and groaning, but maybe just the occasional robin singing for a mate.

It's naïve, and ethereal and crumpled around the edges. It's been around the block. It's here for a good time, not a long time. It lasts and lasts. Longer than chewing gum or batteries.

Have you ever made a roux? It's known as the mother sauce in French cooking. Butter and flour in equal measures. You stir and stir until it turns the colour you're after. It can be an almost dark red, though some recipes call for a lighter roux. When you look it up on the internet, there are a lot of people telling you how to make a *rue*. Which I think would be a different thing altogether. But this line I'm imagining is like a roux, something that emerges from prolonged stirring and mixing and is really very simple.

If you could recreate the single singular dab that Vermeer makes on the bottom lip of the girl with the pearl earring. I guess we all know it wouldn't be the same, alone, lonely on a canvas.

October 15, 1923, Virginia Woolf writes in her diary: "I feel I can use up everything I've ever thought." And I keep having that same feeling, you know, though it rises up in me some mornings, and then will disappear into the dailiness of twenty first century suburban life, or whatever it is you wish to call this life of mine. It's a potent thing. This feeling of artistic culmination, or force, when I realize that all the time I've spent slogging these past decades, actually decades, means something, even if only to me personally. So often filled with fear, and inadequacy, and also at times the struggle of having an outsized ego. The ongoingness, the inspite of. The doubt the questioning and finally just the doing. A tenacious making.

And then I think, well. How long does one keep this feeling, even if it does hide after frothing up. It's not gone far. You can still feel it over there, like you can feel the presence of a child you're looking after, how you know when they're creeping toward the cookie jar or reaching something on a high shelf. So, it's there, but it won't always be there.

Okay, so imagine more than just one brushstroke. Maybe several books in a span of say five, or seven, maybe ten years. And after that, after this sort of culmination where you use up everything, you're drinking so deeply. There's a glow around you, some strange light that emanates from your belly which not everyone can see, but you know, it's there, it's there. Anyway, after this span of time, then what? There's something else, a scaling back, paring down, which is however informed by that culmination, those heady years. Maybe that's when the line comes. The mark.

I've started recognizing these lines in other people's work. Often the writer has to write an entire book around the line. There's a lack of coherence, a critic might say, or people you know and are related to will say things like, oh, that was different.

Do you remember when espresso was first introduced in this town? That's how old I am, I can remember these things. Before Starbucks and Second Cup, there were bistros on Whyte Avenue that put up signs in their windows. They were trying to translate this experience for us, that they'd had back home. Some of the café owners were from Europe and had come here to make a better life. The signs written backwards on the inside of dusty windows by a waiter said, Expresso! Now available. Get it here!

Such passion. Just reading it is like a jolt of caffeine.

Not long after it became common to order a latte. Which if you ordered this in Italy, you'd get a glass of milk. But no matter. I'm not laughing at any of this. At the time, I'd never even heard of espresso, or expresso.

When I was younger, I used to hate it when people said 'take care' as a sort of adieu. What did it really mean? And how could they possibly mean it every time they said it? How did things like that, common phrases, mean? But now I always want to end poems that way.

You, lonely souls, take care, take care.

TREMBLE

I want to get at the strangeness of living in the suburbs. How nothing seems to happen.

I want to contrast this place I live in with the places other artists live in, write from. I don't know if or to what degree landscape is significant. It's always interesting to look at photographs or paintings of a writer's desk, or artists' studios, though, that landscape. And then there are the surrounding landscapes. I'm thinking of the birch trees Paula Modersohn-Becker painted at Worpswede. For Van Gogh, those fields of sunflowers. Giverny for Monet. Hemmingway's Paris. Where we are is so often accidental, though the reasons we stay or move might mean a little something.

One tires of hearing about landscape in Canada. Most of us tune out at the word prairie. Maybe people tune out at the word suburbs, too.

Driving home from the grocery store a couple of days ago there was a man walking down the street carrying a pillow in a floral pillow case. The kind you sleep on. Under his arm. Walking very determinedly down the main road, no sign of turning off. Another day my daughter and I were driving and noticed two young girls walking, but a Mercedes with tinted windows was following them. And they were talking to someone inside while walking. Then they quit talking and continued walking, more hurriedly, and looked annoyed. This made us feel uncomfortable. So we pulled over a couple of blocks ahead and watched in the rearview mirror. Eventually they all stopped at a mailbox a couple of car lengths behind us and were all taking mail out of the same box. The person inside the car appeared to be the mother.

The homeless man riding his bike with four huge, oversized garbage bags, so full, he can't possibly see to ride. But he does, out of the suburbs on garbage day. Cans and bottles, and who knows what.

There is the white, fluffy dog named Happy who barks uncontrollably as though it's in tremendous pain every time a person with a dog walks by the grey fence. And this is on the walking path, where dogs and people walk all day long.

One of our neighbors thinks the noise from the freeway is giving her a nervous breakdown. After living here for twelve years, I'm almost used to it. I hardly notice, especially when I'm writing. When the windows are closed, I can't hear a thing. But she hears everything. The semis that careen by, the motorcycles. The house shakes, she says, it shakes, and inside I'm frayed and shaking too.

In the summer we walk by bus stops smoothly, the dog and I. But during the school year there are often abandoned sandwiches, and the dog lunges and usually eats the thing in one bite. A sandwich left at a bus stop makes me sad on so many levels.

There is a den of coyotes that live in the utility corridor not far behind our house, and on the other side of it is a freeway. One night lying in bed insanely tired, hot, window open, we heard the coyotes yowling directly after several sirens went past. Fire trucks, ambulances. Quite a few. The next day, walking the dog on the path, I saw a young deer running along the tree line in the field that is the utility corridor. This is where the coyotes live – right in the middle of that skinny line of trees, so the walkers of dogs in our neighborhood say. The deer seemed to continue on. I lost sight of it.

All summer long, looking, waiting, noticing.

"In art," says Gauguin, "one idea is as good as another. If one takes the idea of trembling, for instance, all of a sudden most art starts to tremble. Michelangelo starts to tremble. El Greco starts to tremble. All the Impressionists start to tremble."

The sunflower fields tremble and the streets of Paris tremble and the birch forests tremble and the suburbs tremble too.

And I.

CALM

In a world where we are at times blind to each other's transparencies and fragilities and where sorrow may easily permeate soulwings, I wonder what it means to be convinced of the significance of seeking calm. I wonder what it means to contemplate an object or still life in the 21st century. Do we look at things differently than things were looked at in past centuries? How do we see the space around the object and what is our experience of light and darkness? Muddiness? Time?

The Japanese, you might remember, refer to the genre of still life, as "calm things," as compared to the French, "nature morte," or the Italian, "vita silente." This has meant a lot to me, not just because I once wrote about it, but because it changed the way I look, not just at still life, but life. Knowing that the way we refer to a subject changes how we see it. It's a small tilt of the head, but it matters.

Turning an object on a table to meet the light, quietly and deliberately adjusting the position of a teacup, an orange, a bird's nest. I find these gestures to be elegant and rather beautifully fragile. They also remind me of how tenuous things are. And the manner in which things hum, the gorgeously incomprehensible humming of a bowl of summer peaches for example.

The delight in contemplating an object comes first – the shysoftspark. Sometimes a sense of holiness follows. When I was growing up we didn't go to church and I had this funny idea that I was missing out on what was holy, on these depths that the world cradled, hidden and open, and this bothered me and buzzed at my ears in a lament. But I remember sitting on fallen trees in the forest, contemplating nature, a shaving of birch bark and the fringes of certain leaves, tendrils of moss, and trying to become silent inside and still. I remember trying to empty my mind and concentrate on my breath and to let bird song penetrate me. I imagined that my lungs were tentatively open bird cages. And my thoughts were white and soaring having caught a breeze up high on a calm day. In my way, I was free. It was a secret I kept without knowing it was a secret.

I knew nothing about St. Teresa of Avila, Siddhartha, or Rumi. But there is a natural instinct that a body has for tranquility. For serenity.

Space around an object, the way the eye rests on the curves of things – plums, apricots. The distance from a wall and the alteration of shadows in space because of the placement of an object, near or far. The effervescence of light like champagne in the evenings that makes you forget the object you might be contemplating almost entirely. How noticing this erupts into a tingling that may or may not represent a connection to the universe.

It used to be an 'out there' thing to say – that everything is connected, but you come across it in so many places these days it's nearly ordinary. It depends on how long a person is willing to think about an idea and how many permutations they'll take it through as to how meaningful this becomes.

The word 'calm' is said to have come from the Old Italian, "heat of the mid-day sun." We had eaten our shrimp sandwiches and had small bottles of cold white wine and were now propped up against a plinth somewhere in Rome. Our honeymoon, 1993. I can't remember what the statue was atop the plinth, extended high into the sky above with the energy of stone. Just the relaxed languorous, distilled feeling, eyes half open, soothed. In the cool shadow of all the other plinths and their giant unremembered statues.

The Greek root for the word calm means, "to burn." And it's like that too. An inward simmering, summering, down, into oneself. In the heat of the sun, burning, the shade is sought.

I try to think calm thoughts. I have a mantra, words from St. Julian of Norwich, all shall be well and all shall be well and all manner of things shall be well. I make lists, just like Sei Shonagon did in her *Pillow Book* in the year 1000 or thereabouts.

Small towers of grey flat stones as a point of contemplation.
Early evening snow.
Breathing patterns of books overflowing the shelf.
Light through golden leaves.
Jasmine tea.
Stone bowls filled with lovely things, blossoms, leaves.

I have the posture of a woman accustomed to inhabiting chaise longues mainly for the purposes of daydreaming. I would like you to believe that this is an indication of my inner calm but you know that would be a trick of light. When I check my blog statistics there is always at least one person who arrives at "Calm Things" with the search string: "things that are calm." Which makes me feel bad and needlessly self-absorbed for being so random and inconsistent in that space.

I'm just an ordinary heartbroken person searching for things that are calm myself. I have insomnia a few times every month, I have nightmares where I'm too afraid to open my eyes when I awaken. I'm at the age where I realize I have put too much faith in the coin I tossed into the Trevi fountain and I'm suspicious of people who say they don't remember their dreams and so are convinced they don't have any. Maybe because they want to appear to be more real or substantial.

The need to be alone in my mind is sometimes intense and sudden. Which may be interpreted as estranging and it is but empathy can't always correspond to the need or want for it.

One of the first moments of praise for my work included the word, elegant, and it's the only praise I've ever been able to internalize about my writing. So there is this desire underlying everything I write, the desire to live up to this word bestowed upon me.

I'm remembering a dream I had recently where I was trying to arise from my recumbent position on the chaise longue. I was hampered by a set of wings that refused to unfurl because they were birthdamp, mucousy and bloody. I never could get up. So I understand the need to keep dreams inside and yet I see them as paintings I might create in a previous or subsequent life.

Another thing. I very often dream of myself in apartments, some sparse-gloomy and some quite posh, rather than in a house, which is where I live at present. This actually I find stressful even though these apartments might just be from scenes and settings from novels I could write.

Some early mornings I sit on the chaise longue in the upstairs window, my bedroom. The light from the closet is on behind me, and there is a streetlight at the end of the driveway. And I try to burn, to burn a little. I might take my glasses off, and sit and think in the blur and darkness before the sun comes up. And I wonder how that way of seeing changes things too. Beginning the day soft and unfocused but alert and contemplative as well.

Three days in a row, just ordinary days, shifting between knots and paralysis and a curling winding despair. And then, fine. A fine day. Perfectly fine. You know, back to the regular naïve programming, and calm, inner tranquility. It's like that. The world is all in your head at all times but knowing that means you will forget same. But today there are pink roses in a short, clear vase. And I'm here for them. And I believe in them and I believe that they believe in me.

RESIDUE

I wonder what it's possible to say simultaneously open and clandestine and what the choreography of that dance might look like.

When I go to someone's house I'm immediately drawn to their bookshelves, or to a stack of books left out on the coffee table. Most writers inhabit a sort of complicated torment and at times because of various insecurities and the need to slot oneself into a potentially confusing and highly ritualized hierarchy, it can be most interesting to see the order of things and which books are beside or near or placed upon other books.

What I mean to point out is how easy it is to identify those books, the empty ones, the kind you buy to store documents or to secrete money and jewels from thieves.

I have a steel grey cement bird that I bought at Canadian Tire in my garden. The bottom slides out and there is the spot for a key in its paunch. But who would hide a house key there when just the week before there were rows and shelves of them, barcodes reluctantly adhering to the surface of wings, at the store and don't thieves shop at Canadian Tire too? I put the empty bird on top of a stone amid the delphiniums. I have nothing to hide. But the message of the empty bird occupies me all afternoon.

I think of a child standing outside in the cold waiting for a parent to come home. As a child I wore a key around my neck when my mom had to work and now you can buy one on a chain with Swarovski crystals embedded on it for great sums that opens nothing. Though maybe it would be good to be able to open nothing.

Books are becoming obsolete they say and so are keys but there doesn't seem to be as much anxiety surrounding keys.

Some mornings I compose letters elucidating the common motivations of those living in a perpetual state of emergence and distress and hopefulness in my head to Gwyneth Paltrow not just because I'm sympathetic to the assumptions made due to her blonde hair and because sometimes she sends me a newsletter right to my inbox which I don't always have time to read. She's obviously a creative person of excellent taste which is a thousand times too rich for my blood but I appreciate that she shows me things and places that are so delectable and rarified I don't even yearn for them. I can't help but imagine that she's a nice person.

We've painted the house, one room at a time, over four or five months, shades of grey. Quite subtle shifts from room to room, pewter, shale, tempest, but the last one is slate which really speaks to me. We chose grey not so much to match my increasingly winter pale complexion, or to match the shades of my right ventricle or left atrium but as a response to the potential of a mid-life crisis, as response to the fact that I am too many people all at once and because it's impossible to keep track some days so that I feel like I might materialize on another world.

On the day that a literary award is announced, Giller, Griffin, G.G., I tend to write a lot. This particular response to another work of art being recognized for excellence might be seen as a moment of inspiration though it could as easily be construed as spiritual dissolution or jealousy or even as a perverse reaction to the glam futility of a personal pursuit of beauty and understanding through words.

And maybe G.P.'s sense of the beautiful isn't so different from mine, from the sense of beauty I aspire to create. A seeking wondering sharing kind of beauty.

I find it hard to think of Gwyneth and not have the pink, Ralph Lauren Oscar dress conjured as well. She wore it in 1999 at the 71st Academy Awards and it's still being discussed on the internet. Was it a life sized Barbie outfit, or, a concoction befitting a young, talented, Oscar winning, Hollywood star? Delicate flower petal or cotton candy.

Surrounded by and adorned in grey I feel more myself and I have no idea why that is or what it tells you about me that I'd rather, in my introverted solitude-loving state, you not know.

A colour or shade can be significant in ways that might not alter narrative. But details have a way of leaving an impression that resonate and colours can seep into deluxe and unlikely patterns in our imagination.

The love of grey does not preclude a yearning for light. The sky is grey one morning and I feel myself sinking, into that very unpleasant and unproductive winter malaise. The sun began to burn the clouds away into waves like handwriting loops. Long lines of patient practice. An intervention to which I concede.

It's not difficult to see human beings as flowers. Such potential for glory, for magnificence. So much drama in a single slender stem, in the act of blooming, or failing to bloom. Nor is it difficult to imagine people as birds. Grey dove. Flamingo, hummingbird, budgie.

The next thing I want to think about is the surplus value of an image, this thing that W.J.T. calls "the residue," which is all the stuff swirling around an image. The beyond of the image. And also the parts "beyond communication, signification, and persuasion." Free association. The work of art or image as jumping off point, place of inspiration. Without knowing what the residue is when approaching a painting, say, it's still possible to feel a presence. The air thickens around an object, our eyes must adjust to the smoke of what we can't see. Try to remember when you fully understood the expression: breathtaking. It's difficult to say how much we, as viewers in a museum, might experience the localized shards of decades of this phenomena. And then, sharp and dispersed, seeds on an unexpected gust of wind, snowflakes whirring like table saws.

The word glamour is an interesting one. Delusively alluring, says *The Free Online Dictionary*. A glamour, in archaic usage, was a magic spell or enchantment. But has come to be associated with vampires thanks to the recent prevalence in popular culture and is used more frequently as a verb. *The Urban Dictionary* says glamouring is this: The act performed by a vampire to hypnotize humans into submission so they can drink their blood or have control over them.

Stephen Cheeke, in *Writing for Art*, says that we are never unglamoured. That words and images constantly have us in their spell.

Words can be unstable and helpless and fragrant but I don't want this porridge I'm making to be hypnotic even if on the whole it may contain illuminating resonances, soft new colours entering your consciousness. Nor do I wish to drink your blood.

Occasionally,{I write in my letter to G.P.}, though not as often as you might imagine, R. will have finished a painting at about the same time as

I have a piece of writing I'd like him to read. It's a false picture but it's how I like to think of us, however delusive. A glass of red wine in each of our hands, and outside the snow floats around, falls, falls, floats. Which is what is happening this evening in the dark, late November.

The images and words of others sink into me like pink crystal visitations on my tongue whose energy reaches quickly direct into my grey ventricles.

The implications of self-hypnosis are mild and disturbing like dreams of motes in dreary apartments and inconsolable blessings for the enchanted.

COCKTAIL PARTY

I wish my life to flower.

A conversation with an artist at a cocktail party began with a discussion about the studio as a sacred space. Every studio should have a plaque on the door that says, don't come in. Don't even dream about coming in. This is my dream, and I am currently deep in the forest of my dream. Please do not breathe too close to the door because I will feel your presence there.

The artist talks about her connection to paint. The paint is a skin, I say. We go on, back and forth until I'm not sure who has said what. The paint is a skin we say and a painting will have flakes of the skin of the painter, hair pulled from the head, perhaps. One might extract DNA samples from the surface of a painting. It's difficult to part with a work of art for that reason.

The studio is a magic place, holy. Not everyone should tread there. Not every painting should be owned. Some belong purely in a public place where they can be visited when one is in the correct frame of mind – they need to be approached with care, a certain intent, desire for transcendence.

Silence. I don't want to forget that we talked about working in silence. How the wrong word entering into the space of the work can damage it, damage us.

The artist is pulled away to meet one of the buyers of her latest works. I own your painting, says the buyer. Repeats this three times. I own, I own, I own. But I renamed it. I renamed it because I think the subject of the work is not what you say it is. It is this other thing that I will tell you about at great and piteous length.

We are smiling and our eyes are meeting.

At another party I hear someone say, I hate poetry.

But I don't have a context for that line so I'm going to pretend that they meant to say, I wish I had more poetry in my life because I wish my life to flower. I wish to feel flowers when I walk by a shop in the mall, fragrant and fresh. I don't know this person but I admit the words haunt me and hurt me, and make me tremble a little when I think of them. I know someone who constantly inserts the phrase, *I don't care*, with a certain vehemence into her conversations, and it affects me in a similar way.

The artist says that her mother is a witch and she has asked her to cast a fierce spell on a particular painting so that it won't be purchased.

The morning after this party I take out my copy of the Joseph Campbell book with the hundred dog ears. He talks about the Grail quest and how he Holy Grail is a symbol of ' the highest spiritual fulfillment of a human life." It's easy to stray from the path of your own quest, to take up another's path, to stray. When you're doing the thing you're supposed to be doing and when you're surrounded by the right people, when you're fulfilled, you're in the Grail Castle. Campbell says that the quickest way to lose the Grail is "to go to a cocktail party."

He also says that *art is the set of wings to carry you out of your own entanglement* and at times it's meaningful to trace your finger over that invisible flight you may have taken one day in the middle of winter, the sky so deep and grey you can only breathe the word forgive.

ANOTHER COCKTAIL PARTY

Three of us talking at the cocktail party for the visiting artist. Talking about an artist from our city who moved to a bigger fancier city.

X is successful, X is Someone, because X moved away, is one person's view.

Which is a statement I back away from, I literally take a step backwards.

And it makes me tired straightaway so that my eyelids turn into cement, I adopt the pose of statuary. It's nothing I haven't heard before, variations on the theme come up often. I want to talk about how complicated moving away is, what we would be leaving, about friends I have that make me ache with their beauty, and about the new job I have that I love and that allows me to write and think, uncluttered and happy, and about how dear it is to me that my kid is content in school.

But the person goes on for a while about the subject of artists and how they can't grow unless they break free from this place we happen to live, where we lean toward existence.

Why is it that so often we do not honor or nurture or even acknowledge those among us who are visionaries, and poets, and dreamers?

The third person in the group, gratifyingly, quotes my husband, at present across the room, who has said that if one were to live in a beautiful village in Italy, one would walk to the store that sells bread every day, past an exquisite fountain in the piazza. For the first one hundred or so days you would look intently and with awe at the fountain, but after that, it would just be going to the store to get the bread. And that wherever one is, working, painting, mainly you exist in the harmonious and unsettling mystification which is the making of art.

The first person forgot who I was for a second, that my artist husband and I have chosen to stay. Or it wasn't forgotten. At times people feel it's their duty to tell you the error of your way. And I let them. In lieu of telling them theirs.

In lieu, because I'm often failing trying to become kinder. And because I'd prefer my poems be a space for working things through rather than exacting a petty sort of revenge, or taking a shot at someone behind their back. So you see what I mean about failing trying.

FEIGNING

I smiled wanly at the art critic's joke attempting to conceal my pity.
Don't worry, he says.

I want to use an adverb here, to create a balance with the use of the word
'wanly.' Maybe *archly* or *superciliously*. But I decide against it. Because
it doesn't matter how he says this.

He says, don't worry.
You'll get it when you're back at home.

And I pretend not to get that either. Best to go forward in this way.
Bigger fish to fry, he walks away in his sad trousers with a sort of
lopsided, self-rapturous, peach eating grin, so in love with himself. And
I'm happy for him. I notice he walks around for a time trying to exude
mysteriousness while everyone else in the room studiously avoids him.

I have this quotation pinned up near my desk by the 7th century Chinese
Chan Buddhist Master, Hongren: "Work, work! ... Don't waste a
moment . . . Calm yourself, quiet yourself, master your senses. Work,
work! Just dress in old clothes, eat simple food…feign ignorance, appear
inarticulate. This is most economical with energy, yet effective."

What I tried to get when I was back at home had more to do with things
like: the need some people have to practice staking out a territory even
when the territory to be had is strictly and even poorly imagined. More
importantly I attempted to work out how it's possible to feel generous
toward someone with that particular need before I returned to my work
consisting of absorbing transcendent theories of wintering.

TRANSACTIONS WITH BEAUTY

When you're writing dialogue, you must keep in mind the way most people listen, often sideways. One person says one thing, and the other one tells you about what they have to do that day because it floods them with equal measures of anxiety and self-importance. She started to tell me about the pork chops at Costco so suddenly and at such length that I'm still astonished.

I once went for coffee with a woman who was always punctually late, because, she actually confessed this to me, she didn't like to be kept waiting. She then proceeded to adoringly talk about herself and ask for advice about her problems for two hours and then at the end, maybe as we were standing to leave, as a way to deflect from the scantiness of the tip she left, would say, so what's new with you, nothing then? And this would be impossible to answer.

I also still find that astonishing twenty years later.

In an interview with Paul Auster, Edmond Jabes mentions that always, when two people talk, one must be silent. The longer the one person talks, the more questions are formed in the mind of the listener, but these questions are eliminated as the speaker goes on.

I have been trying, as Pascal said, to always keep something beautiful in my mind. As a way of righting myself, as a way of balancing things out. Balancing the pork chops with the way the sky changes in a sigh from a smoky purple to a light pink and how the snow gathers that into its deceptive smoothness, as creamy as a can of Betty Crocker icing.

And what to do with those discarded questions that have been turned into wisps and smoke rings?

The thing is I do like to listen. Some conversations are like long exposure photographs that allow you to see into time. Others are cats walking down the sidewalk at 3am, only their eyes visible. When you listen you begin to understand that each conversation has its own architecture, sometimes it's like Gaudi and sometimes it's like the Eiffel Tower or the Leaning Tower of Pisa.

When you're writing poetry, it's good to think of Sappho and her brilliant shards. To imagine, as Rachel Blau Duplessis has said, that only a smudged line, or creased fragment might survive. So write every line as if it is that fragment.

And it's not a shard but these lines by Rumi are true:

Lovers find secret places
inside this violent world
where they make transactions
with beauty.

The trouble for me is when so many voices are rattling and making ruins in my head that I forget to make those delicate and at times sacrificial transactions and that the secret place is *now* in the way that clouds are now.

"Beauty is nothing other than the promise of happiness," Stendhal pointed out, and whoever quotes him these days is usually quick to point out that promises are so often broken. Well. You can see why beauty has to go underground.

I can say that I'm happier on those days when I've made clandestine transactions with beauty, hidden ones. Like the messages received in spy movies, the ones that self-destruct in five seconds.

"A thing of beauty is a joy for ever," the opening line of Keats's *Endymion*. Which is a message that hasn't self-destructed, whatever we think of it. In the movie about Keats and Fanny Brawne, Keats is made to say, "Poetry soothes and emboldens the soul to accept mystery." Which is lovely, even if Keats himself didn't quite say it. Because the soul does need to be emboldened to accept mystery, it needs to listen deeply to the universe, the mystery, and that's not an easy place to get to.

The consumptive Keats, sent to Italy against his wishes, too weak to argue, continued to decline. He and his friend took up residence in a flat just above the Spanish Steps. He'd tried to overdose himself, he'd stopped eating. When offered a plate of spaghetti, fare he was unaccustomed to, he managed to get to the window in a rage and threw it out, so it landed on the Spanish Steps. Another sort of transaction with beauty.

I don't mind if beauty breaks promises, even very often, so long as the promises continue to be made. I won't mind if beauty arrives late or talks about pork chops. And I'm even willing to see that the act of the spaghetti being thrown out the window onto stairs unscalable by a consumptive, soon to perish, 26 year old who had contributed so vastly to the beauty of this often violent and ugly world of ours, was a sort of mad, whirling, beautiful thing to do. A feast for the pigeons. A beautiful mess, after all.

Questions? Who knows what will survive.

OH HOW IT LOVES YOU

To prove that you were never even remotely ordinary I would make a film that would follow the light from your childhood all the way through your life, in and out of windows, through corridors, in the backyard, down the street, and falling on your hands as you washed the breakfast dishes in solemnly radiant bubbles. I would follow the line of light like a poem, flowing from stanza to stanza, from room to room, through your life and into the lives of those you love and who love you.

When others come to see this movie they're going to be expecting it to be sappy, but it's not, because light is more hardy than that; it sustains and it illuminates but it exacts nothing from anyone. It is so much. Even so, there are those who will get up and leave muttering about how nothing happens and that there's no story, and how they've been ripped off and want their money back. But the movie is free, and the only catch is you have to navigate dimly down a back alley at night to get to the theatre. (Do you remember reading a scene in a book something like that, and there's a neon light, at the end of a long alley?) The thing is they want to leave because they haven't noticed the light in the movie at all, its starring role. They just see strange details of boring things, odd croppings, strange angles and unjustified close-ups and they note an absence of Hollywood actors and explosions.

It begins with the light that collects in the landscape of your sheets and rests in the indentation on your pillow on a summer morning like leftover dreams. A clean, club soda light.

The light sweeps and whispers through laundry on a line and the white sheets wave and billow until the shape of a wing appears and the camera freezes that for a few seconds, just long enough to leave the viewer with an intense desire to see it again.

It illuminates the reddish winter coat of a horse, and then she moves her head into the light, so her whiskers are apparent. And you move your hand into that light, and the horse blows on your palm, a sun kissed benediction. You've remembered that your whole life, haven't you?

A woman sits in a car, waiting for her child to come out of school, and she has rolled the window down. The sun strikes the side of her cheek and unconsciously, she leans toward it, into it, so that her neck and shoulders are at odd angles. A bird flies overhead, between the sun and her cheek. The breathlessness of that moment, small, wondrous.

Late at night, a computer screen filled with mathematical formulas, a strict and quivering light.

Light dives like a swallow into a glass of champagne. Such accuracy and surprise.

The skinned and haloed light in a birthing room. There is the sickly hospital light but set that aside. This is replaced by the new life and all the miraculous energy it takes to birth. You'll remember this as the one moment you were completely sure there is a god.

Maybe there is a scene, in the middle of the night when the phone rings and you turn on the light to answer the phone, fumbling and groggy. You sit up and swing your legs over, feet on the floor, toes digging into the carpet. The light from your bedside table makes your legs and feet look yellow and as you begin to shake, the light flutters, reminds you of being rocked back and forth, back and forth by the light itself.

Did I mention I would like my film of you to be an homage to Beckett, to the fact that he could write so much darkness and yet produce such startling light. I want it to be a rope that you follow from the farm house in a severe and relentless snowstorm to the barn so that you may feed the starving animals.

This is maybe my favorite part of the film. There is a kitchen table scene, a very grey day, so that the light is straining and shabby. You know it loves you then. Oh, how it loves you.

It's mid-day and there's tea and a plate of biscuits, store bought ones, and everyone is happy. But the frame is centered on the table, there are hands reaching, lifting cups. All you see is the way the light reaches and holds the scene together. And the light modulates, first it is very weak, then a little less weak. Someone picks up a crumb with a forefinger, that gesture. Someone else has folded their hands. After quite a long time, there is an opening in the grey sky, or it is considerably less grey, and so the scene changes dramatically. Although nothing has changed. A cup is raised, an elbow is placed on the table. Someone leans in. The flowers on the teacups swagger and glint and the limpid tea is now a magical, tremulous pond. The sugar on the cookies is now sequined and glorious. But then the grey light returns, swings in hard left, a light in which everyone is from another year, not old, not young, but who they are. Only different and enlivened and bright. So beautifully bright.

The movie goes on for hours, with free popcorn and orangina, showing how one person may be ensouled through a continued experience with the frequencies and wavelengths and blossomings of light.

A SONNET

Driving home at night, following the full moon back to the suburbs from downtown, after something I didn't exactly wish to do in the first place. I remember the list of things she said had recently made her cry, and the list became a sort of unholy mantra in my head, and I held it in my mouth like a freshly unfurled spring blossom.

She said weep, actually, rather than cry. It occurs to me that I weep all the time, never with tears, but silent, dry and deep inside, so that my shoulders barely shake. When I write my autobiography I'll elaborate on this, but for now you can imagine it has to do with a visceral reaction to the vibrant colours of cut flowers.

I write the first draft of this in my Volkswagen Jetta, turning into this particular sprawl of the suburbs, driving slowly then, slower, alone under the streetlights drowning the moonlight.

I'd like to say something important just as much as the next poet.

The second draft I write in the bathtub. Naked fluid flawed. Not waving.

Driving home to the comfortable suburbs in the freshly dirty snow, the signs in red and white seem aglow, seem to seek my attention. Warnings. Seasonal parking bans. In the snow-filled dry pond, a warning of floods. Green power boxes half buried in snow achieve prominence.

I think of something I once read comparing amplified people to dampened people. How amplified people feel, hear, sense, so much more. They are all nerve endings tingling with the unrecognizable and continuous energy of the world. I keep writing the word, *amplified*, in my journal, as a reminder or a sort of blessing to the dreams that pour out of me.

One day I spend an hour in which I appear to be looking out the window at the bright snow falling, but am instead thinking about the silence of paintings and how the light reflected from snow makes my eyelashes hurt. The conversations that paintings seem to have with each other through time, and with resistant and intermittently radiant, mortals. The one that always begins, "I have seen this."

The waiting we're all doing, sucking on cough drops, a mentholyptic quiet.

Another draft is written during my morning walk with the dog. It's nearing the end of winter and so the snow is older, crystallized, tired. I walk by the awkward stand of trees that no one thought to chop down, at least not yet, and a swirl of small birds rises up and hits the sky like it's Broadway, like another day at the office. Even though the sky is dark grey, I see it in pastel gradations, light green, cotton candy pink, and blue Kool-Aid.

This, just as I'd been mentally replaying the scene in the movie where Julia Roberts comes home from teaching a class at the local college and starts blending a slushy, lime margarita that she then drinks from an enormous glass. The movie is about how when you're uninspired, you end up being uninspiring in tandem with what to do when you've been downsized by a soulless department store, in the case of the Tom Hanks character. But all I can think about is I wish I were that gorgeous when getting wasted on forgetting and disappointment.

That writing poetry is a mode of seeking inspiration or a relentless pursuit of the ideas of others.

Another draft of this is written on the chaise longue, upstairs window. Feeling hypochondriacal and unphotogenic and vague. Blanket on my lap. Shivering. I copy poems of others into my journal as a way into their cadences. Inhabiting briefly. I go on to peruse an essay by one of these venerable poets, the young ones are chastised. There is not enough at stake in their poems, he says.

I want to write sparely with clarity and wisdom but also long messy lines cryptic and covert.

I hold this poem up to the poems I love, all those patient, reckless syllables. And maybe it gives up too soon. After all, it has this in common with every poem, it says, *love me*. And in common with all the paintings, it says, *see this along with me*.

There are drafts after this draft, as well, where the poem is whittled down and contorted and caressed and whispered into, until it assumes the thirsty shape of a sonnet or a margarita glass.

VIDEO ART

He's not habitual.

So if I set up a camera at the end of my street to try to capture his passing by at the same time everyday, there would be a lot of footage recording his absence.

The enclave of the suburbs where both he and I are situated is centered around a dry pond. A walk around the circle takes approximately 25 minutes at a leisurely pace.

In the winter he wears a black coat and a black tuque. In the summer he wears a black t-shirt.

He has a splendid black moustache and when he walks he seems to be leaning back, into his own existence, comfortable.

In his left hand there is always a cigarette, held low, held close.

The trail of ash, invisible evidence, poetry.

His entrance into my field of vision is always at a different point of the circle.

He doesn't litter. I've seen him putting the cigarette stub into the cement garbage container by the bus stop on more than one occasion.

Sometimes I spot him when I drive by in my grey car. But I've passed him walking, too. He says hello but he doesn't have to break into a smile, because he's always smiling.

Once he said, you have a fine black dog. And another time, your dog is a lovely good creature.

I saw him yesterday on the opposite side of the street and he nodded.

Cordial. Which you'll understand is rare in the suburbs. And in the same interval eight or nine robins, the first of this spring, arise from the bare branches of a tree on his side of the street, and alight upon a tree on my side of the street.

BEWILDERMENTS

"Any one who has common sense will remember that the bewilderments of the eyes are of two kinds, and arise from two causes, either from coming out of the light or from going into the light, which is true of the mind's eye, quite as much as of the bodily eye; and he who remembers this when he sees any one whose vision is per-plexed and weak, will not be too ready to laugh; he will first ask whether that soul of man has come out of the brighter light, and is unable to see because unaccustomed to the dark, or having turned from darkness to the day is dazzled by excess of light." - Plato

It was early in spring and my eyes were still adjusted for winter.

All winter I did reference work on bewilderments. I filled stone bowls with flower petals which I placed by the window on days when snow fell and tried to describe the colour of them throughout the course of the day. At times it was easier to see the colours within this sparse indifferent season or, the silence let me experience an immersion into the fragility and feverishness of colour out of time. At other intervals still, I was dissolved by the inexactitude of seeing, baptized in that particular and juicy juncture of unknowing.

Sometimes when I took the dog for a walk I would forget to wear my sunglasses and the snowbrightness would become too much and I'd walk with my eyes closed for a spell.

It was early in spring one night after dinner and I made sour cherry cupcakes with the fruit we'd frozen last year from the tree in the backyard remembering how it blossomed last year, how abundant the fruit was, and how we'd left some for the birds but now the tree was bare. I remember balancing on a ladder in the middle of the branches, plucking fruit, looking up, squinting into the glittering green to find more.

The light was going and normally I wouldn't have even tried to photograph anything, but I clicked away in spite of that, thinking how little I know about the light, about 'capturing' it. And how I want to stretch myself, and to look more closely, and also from further away. I want to know more about the interaction of shadows and distance and how negative space is a gasp whether it holds light or darkness.

How quickly the dark comes down upon us.

And yet, still it's possible to find slivers of light. To push the table closer to the window angled toward the setting sun.

Are we coming out of the light, or going into the light?
And likewise, when we meet someone, have they come from a place of light or from a place of darkness? How to steady them as their eyes adjust?

How to steady ourselves?

COMPENSATIONS

The day in April when I shot photos of snow just beginning to melt on the not quite emerging leaves along the gray fence where I walk the dog is also when I see someone being taken out of a house on a stretcher in a body bag. The cop cars, facing the same direction, one on each side of the street, drive away at the same time and at first I think they're going to side-swipe each other.

Two men in black suits slide the stretcher with the black body bag into a clean, grey mini-van. When they drive away, merge into the suburbs, it reminds me of an airplane taking off. Something earthbound is surrounded by air and is removed from us and without meaning to I shrug my shoulders.

My entire walk in the melting snow, I wonder how we avoid colliding with each other, how easy it is to disguise an event that must have broken at least one or two mortal hearts.

When I get back home I read the Zagajewski poem about literary rats. And I think about how most of us are passed over by our contemporaries, and at times feel their derision, though this might be wishful thinking. Mostly we hang out at the Oblivion Café, located near the far end of a large country. That's okay, the coffee is good, and they serve wine in the late afternoon.

There will be literary betrayals. We all know that, too.

It's quite possible to smile at the people who sold you out, right after calling in a favor you didn't owe, and once in a while you have a drink with one of them. The betrayals seem carefully constructed and executed to resemble obliviousness. I find them difficult to forgive because we who create know what a delicate state it's necessary to inhabit for long stretches, as we wait to accept magic, which is how Balthus described what it was to live in the sacred world of painting.

She waited to accept magic. And sometimes it arrived.

I'd like someone to say that about me at the end, discrete, before the grey mini-van comes.

People read what you've written and can't help but forget it, or forget to associate those words and feelings with who you are, or neglect to place it in the context of how breakable each of us are. Oh, but there are compensations, too, for all that shabby neglect and betrayal you're sure to experience.

You'll sit in the window for hours, you'll be discrete, too. You'll choose magic, you'll accept it, and furthermore, you'll attain silence, you'll come to know the generosity of solitude

ALOOF, ALIGHT, ALOFT

The art auction fundraiser coincided with my 46th birthday and so we made ourselves fancy and I put on my only pair of high heels, low, black ones, and met some friends there. It was a good party, cooler music than I'm used to, and louder. Pale champagne offered at the top of three flights of stairs. Trays of cute things to eat.

After a few hours of attempting to insert cocktail chatter into the loud music with a shy voice, and circling back to the donated painting finally relieved that the humiliation of eliciting no bids is averted, I am overcome with the need to escape, and we leave without saying goodbye to our friends. My triangulated toes are on fire inside my beautiful Italian shoes for which I received many compliments.

The next morning walking the dog I see the black pump, not mine, discarded in the newly green grass. It had rained, just the smallest amount, and there was dew in the grass, and also on the black shoe.

I'm not sure about the significance of the detail of the black shoe in the tender grass and am reminded of the advice that's always given to writers starting out. That you may have to sacrifice that part of the writing you hold most dear, or worked on the most, because it's extraneous, or incongruous, and that you have to be ruthless. Ruthless. For the sake of your art. And it doesn't matter that you're haunted by something like a black pump on the edge of a lawn in the suburbs and the speed and velocity and mood in which it was discarded. You have to cast these things off. Excise.

I'm not sure about one person's evaluation of the insignificance of details in poems or in uninterpretable dreams.

There was a freshness. Next I saw birds perched on the very tops of trees. What makes them do that? To hold on, cling to the world, so high up?

When I get to the field, the utility corridor by the highway, I let the black dog loose and we're alone out there. He takes off, nose to the ground, and when he gets pretty far I whistle and he looks up. I use the hand signal he's mostly trained to answer – the outward arm drawn in toward the heart. Always, the possibility he might not come in, the possibility he'd make a bid for freedom, the open road. But he does, this time, circling inward, back, cleverly, quickly.

After, we saunter back down the gravel path toward the streets, the sidewalks. And I enjoy the sun trickling down through the barely unfurled leaves. Thinking about how I always seem to hold myself back from spring these days. How long has this been going on?

Long enough that it seems engrained, but not so long I don't recall what it feels to embrace it – to let the green seep into one, the colour bringing you back to life, your own life. Feeling alive. As if you weren't before. Maybe this is what happens when you've pledged allegiance to winter and the silence and the white too long.

I'm uneasy with my distrust of what seems undeniable and hopeful.

Later, I wonder if there's a word for holding yourself away from spring, aloof. Maybe there is, but instead I find the word: *komorebi*, which means: *sunlight that filters through the leaves of the trees*.

And it doesn't matter, then, if I hold myself back, away, aloof. It will pour down on me anyway, bathe me, the sun, through the leaves, generous glitter and trickle.

IF YOU'RE A POET

The poets I know we talk about this every time a new book comes out. How difficult it is to reconcile the time you spend alone writing, and carving out that enormous space required, so you can *receive* – with the need to perform for an audience.

The days I contrive to behave like a poet are few and far between, even though my entire existence leans toward a window in the hermitage.

Like Van Gogh, I have been trying to get at something utterly heartbroken through my art, through words, for over two decades. The only thing I can honestly claim is that I've had my heart broken by poetry, by this writing life, numerous times.

Is it possible to be a poet these days and not be an academic also? Not just because of the need to make a living, but because otherwise it's all too possible to achieve the dream of reclusivity.

In *Franny and Zooey*, there's the conversation Franny has with Lane over martinis at Sickler's. She's feeling lousy which is why the name of the place is so crazy right. Only Salinger could get away with calling a place Sickler's. Anyway. Franny is saying how the poets in the English Department aren't really poets. It's a good conversation, you should read it. What she says is they're not poets because they don't leave anything that's beautiful. She says,

"If you're a poet, you do something beautiful."

When she's breaking down, right before everything becomes clear, maybe it becomes clear. Zooey, her brother, says to her:

"An artist's only concern is to shoot for some kind of perfection, and on his own terms, not anyone else's."

I get shivers when I read that. It does something to me, to my nerves and I could really use a martini.

So the book has been on my desk for a while. I keep opening to those two pages, one at the front of the book, the other near the back. It's a good enough mantra: if you're a poet, you do something beautiful.

If you're a poet, you do something beautiful.

How difficult it is to say something with such perfect clarity, such truth.

It's nothing against the poets who are also in English Departments. I just know that I couldn't be a poet in an English Department. Of course, it's possible, just not for me.

I'd figured a few things out somehow, hit my stride, in my own way, when I was doing my undergrad degree. I was actually on fire at a certain point, aglow with a strange transformation, metamorphosis. Something out of Star Trek.

It was near the end of the last year and I was walking down the long hallway in the cement building with a friend. His marks weren't as good as mine and he'd been rejected from the poetry classes, but he wrote, all the same, and I'd read a fair bit of his work, his poetry, more brash than beautiful. A professor ran down the hall after him, calling his name, and began admonishing him for not getting his applications in to grad school. There was still time, and she, begging and fawning, convinced him to go, and wrote letters of reference for him.

I remember feeling a little jealous that no one was sprinting down the hallway after me. No one mentioned grad school to me, no one fawned, and why should they, I was too shy, too shy.

The hypothetical question where you're asked to name a figure from literary history you'd like to have dinner with always stresses me out.

First I start thinking about what I'd wear, what could I possibly eat, sitting across from Virginia Woolf or Clarice Lispector or Jane Austen? Maybe we could just have a glass of wine. Or a martini.

I suppose there are those people who'd choose J.D. Salinger. The challenge of the notably reclusive.

Maybe I'll choose Salinger, too. And then I'd let him off the hook. I'd excuse myself, somewhat inarticulately. Because, whatever kind of beauty I'm able to crack open, it's going to be on my own terms. And we'd both want to get back to the work of shooting for perfection, however imperfectly.

RECURRING DREAM

My desire to be intellectually sophisticated and elegant is nearly equal to my desire to be naïve and wild.

These desires must all be hung up to dry as I go off to work. Happily enough, I should add, happily enough.

Only once every month or two do I allow myself to pine. First, I take the word *pine* out of the rusty cage I keep it in and admire it. The word alone touches me and reminds me of spacious collapsing forests and the particular sound of the wind as it moves through evergreen needles.

Betsy Warland has written that we as writers cannot afford to pine for the dream of being able to create full time. Which is so true it can be identified as a flash resembling the light one often sees before the onset of a numbing headache.

Whatever it is you do besides writing or making art, it's important to do it with joy even if it's a complicated joy weighed down by the setting aside of the soul's choreography and is at times mysteriously and disappointedly misconstrued as satisfaction and fulfillment.

A couple of years ago I saw a photograph on the internet of a tree as captivating as the ones you draw in childhood, the branching out even and perfectly spaced and the sturdy trunk situated in a field all by itself except for the one or two daisies. The tree was full of birdcages, maybe a hundred of them, which I soon realized were all the same birdcage, just photoshopped in.

Maybe it was this photograph, my yearning to recreate something similar, that led to my recurring dream all last winter. In the dream, I need to learn how to use Photoshop by the next day, it's a life and death situation, and so I'm up all night trying to master the program. I wake up thinking, quick, I need to download Photoshop and get to work.

When the spring blossoms arrived, I took all the birdcages I have outside and had our daughter help me hang them in the cherry tree. I was happy with the results of the photographs I took and the recurring dream has for now subsided.

There's the poem by Hafiz in which the small person builds cages for everyone, but the wise one nonchalantly drops keys in the moonlight, for the beautiful, unruly prisoners to find.

When I show anyone my photograph of the birdcages in the blossoming tree, I tell them, the doors are open, no locks. This morning I looked outside where I left one of the cages hanging. The air was full of birdsong and one little bird had perched on the top of the cage before disappearing into the sky.

Next year I'll pick up the keys I keep finding and hang them on the tree for anyone to take.

GUERILLA GARDENING

And I'd like to send this one out to all the women who stopped writing and went somewhere else in their heads and their hearts.

Maybe they took up a brush or a camera or moved to Africa. I know I'm tempted to do just that every once in a while. To not think about all the charts and graphs highlighting the ways in which women writers are overlooked that are at long last proliferating and bless the souls who painstakingly accumulated data representing the neglect we had all internalized and experienced. Let's not forget to remember Tillie Olsen in all this, her book, *Silences*, which so many of us have thumbed through for over fifty years.

Sometimes I do stop writing, I do pick up a camera. I used to very badly want to paint and sometimes I did. But it's too late for that, at least for now. It might not be too late later. I can't say.

I can't even begin to tell you what spending ten years, off and on, (and you know it's always off and on) working on a book about a possible woman art forger, about anonymity and hiddenness, and how to disappear, and then having it rejected six ways to Sunday, has done to my psyche. I'm fine with the alterations though, the strange twitches I developed, and my predilection for standing near walls, near doors, open windows.

I used to keep my eye out for those poems women will write where they talk about their rooms, where they write, how this might connect them to other women in their rooms. Often a nod to Virginia Woolf. Often a reference to the money. It still comes back to that, possibility does. Possibility will.

It's the details that always get me in these poems. A description of bruised light, a vase of daisies, a plate with a crust leftover from a cheese sandwich. And very often there's a cup of coffee or tea, sometimes drained, sometimes gone cold. A sign that we are desperate or determined or just hopeful that we can stay awake long enough to get a few things down, to rough them out, lay them down like an underpainting.

Last night there was rain, and this morning I stuffed all the leftover seeds that we didn't have room to plant in the garden into my pocket. I walked out into the utility corridor a bit and planted them, digging down with a stick I found. I did the same thing last spring, planting sunflower seeds. I was happy to see a few of them come up, flower. I walked by them a couple of times before they disappeared. This year I almost didn't want to plant anything out there. The idea of guerilla gardening suddenly seemed childish.

My friend Iman tells the story of packing her books when she was moving from Cairo to North America. Every day she kept trying to reduce the number of books. Of the few that she's able to bring, one is just a sheaf of photocopies of poems by her favorite poet.

As writers we worry so much about typos, what our book will look like, if the text will be reverently and harmoniously placed on the page, and what the cover image will be and how we can present ourselves in an author photo so we are recognizable yet also romantically incorrigible and fabulous looking.

What we should dream about is having our work so well loved that it's photocopied and tied up with recycled twine with the reader's favorite poems at the top, most worn.

When I'm asking you to accept these poems I've written, it's as a work that's leading up to something else and I don't know yet precisely what will be.

Imagine you are sitting outside on your front stoop, waiting for someone inside to wake up. You are twirling a flower between your thumb and forefinger and the person inside is only vaguely in your consciousness, even though your experience is that of someone waiting patiently.

LIBRARY FOR BIRDS

Last night I had this dream I wanted to tell you about but because we've lost touch with each other, *we've lost touch* is the way to say it, speaks to the delicacy in human relationships, I couldn't pick up the telephone or email you.

I couldn't phone you so I thought I'd write a poem in case you still read what I write, in the corner of a bookstore or the public library. I imagine you standing in the 819s while you read, putting the book back on the shelf, in exactly the spot it came from.

The dream was one of those realistic dreams, more realistic than most. I'm still not sure that it wasn't real, or maybe it felt that real because you had the dream as well. July 30, 2012. In case you record such things and want to look back at your notes. I'm kidding, I guess, I'm pretty sure you wouldn't record your dreams. But you should you know, maybe you should.

I dreamed we were friends again. Which isn't possible, or hasn't been, because, distance, time, small misunderstandings on both sides, at least I feel they must be small, I hope, and I'm sorry if they're larger than I have imagined and if I've been completely daft, but mainly because of paths. Things chosen, things given up.

Still, the dream was a comfort, completely tranquil. As though we'd made a kind of peace with all that. In the dream we were just sitting, shoulder to shoulder, smiling at some old joke, something we'd once laughed heartily about under the streetlights on a winter night, the warmth of that time.

In the dream, we were sitting on a bench beside this library I'd read about, the library for birds, built in a forest outside of Beijing. The exterior of the building is constructed from wood from the forest, and the expectation is that birds will begin to nest and the structure will blend ever more harmoniously with its surroundings.

People think that dreams need to be subject to stern and capricious interpretation but this can be an intrusion into private understandings, into what is tender and what is prized for exactly what has been.

We were just sitting comfortably shoulder to shoulder, wing to wing, old friends, earthbound, serene, watching the birds fly by with twigs and treasures and bits of mud.

And I was about to tell you about how I had taken up cataloguing light in my backyard and by the bright window in my kitchen, when the dream quietly ended.

Leave a note here, tucked into this page, if you like, if you have anything at all you want to convey, dreams or remembrances, and I'll get back to you as soon as I can.

WRITING PROMPTS

WRITING PROMPTS

Write a poem about your favorite song, the twang of it, the low notes.
Write a poem about your childhood pet. Your favorite colour. Love gone
wrong. Unrequited love. An epiphany. About the time you fainted in the
museum. Write about an object you lost. About a recurring dream.
Write a poem using the word crepuscular. Write about someone you
hate using the word tenderly. Someone you saw at the mall or you were a
passenger in a car on the highway which slowly passed another car and
you locked gazes with the person in the backseat. Write about snow
melting, an argument you once had, about stargazing, about giving up.
Write about taking the train or the bus and the barbecue chips you ate
while looking at the scenery. Write a poem about a Shakespeare play or
about a movie you saw with someone with whom you are no longer
friendly. Write about how jealous you are of that poem by the more
famous poet. Write about being drunk. Write about the staff lottery pool
and the week you didn't buy in. Write a conversation between two poets
from distant time periods. Write about a conversation Jane Austen
would have with Jane Eyre, a conversation Charlotte Bronte would have
with Elizabeth Bennet. Write a poem about Cary Grant allusions in the
work of Michael Ondaatje beginning with *North by Northwest*. Write a
poem about a house you once lived in, about a house you want to live in,
write about a nest. Write a poem about a book you haven't read. Write
about breakfast, the sound of eggs cracking. Write about what makes
you come alive and about a bird that flew over you, casting its shadow on
the page. Write about a personal slight, about a misunderstanding.
Write about summer. Write about the weather. Write about Virginia
Woolf's dog Flush. Write about candy or a birthday cake. About
patience and solitude using a random word from the dictionary such as,
insufficient. Write a poem about an old photograph, write a poem about
a painting, in the form of a letter, in the form of a postcard. Write a self-
portrait, tell me what you love, tell me about the room in which you
write. Write about writing. Write about sitting in a café and make me fall

in love with that moment. Write about the objects on your desk. Write about what you saw on the news last night and write about celery about soup about your grocery list about Marie de Antoinette, the Marx Brothers, Charlie Chaplin, Greta Garbo, Ingrid Bergman. Write a poem to accompany a silent film. Write a single poem using all the aforementioned writing prompts. Write a poem about writing prompts.

WRITE A POEM ABOUT YOUR DAY

– Each day is precious because each day is essentially the microcosm of your whole life. (John O'Donohue)

The domestic as a point of departure. As good as any place to contemplate the fullness of existence. The notebook moves from the kitchen table to the outdoor table, to the study, to the bedside table. I move from the kitchen sink, from the stove, to the notebook, to the garden. I walk the dog. I notice birds, leaves, the scent hanging in morning air. I move from this chore to that one. I fulfill social obligations, family ones, I love, I wonder, I avoid, I am thwarted. I wash the floor, I vacuum, I prepare, I lunch, I buy groceries. I make sure we are ready. I load the dishwasher, I make dinner, I photograph, I am interrupted, I look out windows. I look at a screen, I blog. I look at Facebook, I sign out, I sign in. I write, I coax words, I open, I prod, I make wishes on butterflies, read the glistening and gorgeous and wild words of others. I breathe and I look and I daydream the mysteries and sincere intoxications of living.

WHAT I LOVE

– after lines by Fanny Howe,
"I won't be able to write from the grave / so let me tell you what I love."

I love drab birds and in winter I love the trees, sugar frosted.
Coffee and milk. Moss in the forest, the cool shady spots where it grows.
Morning light. Pink-apricot rose petals.
Daughter's smile. So many poems.
Leather sandals. Pale blue sky. Suitcases. Home.
The chair in my garden where I can sit and no one can see me.
Daydreaming and nightdreaming -

and poemdreaming.

LIGHT CAN BE

"Light can be gentle, dangerous, dreamlike, bare, living, dead, misty, clear, hot, dark, violet, springlike, falling, straight, sensual, limited, poisonous, calm and soft." – Sven Nykvist

And light can also be wintered, compassionate, worried, filled with birdsong and jasmine tea, sharp, worried, slight, revealing, watery, curious, blue.

Light can be mild, cutting, still, flickering, unswerving, bewildering, slanted, easy, difficult, smudgy, foggy, soothing, divine, muscular, oblique, buttery, flimsy, relentless, unasked for, ordinary, inspiring, indefinite.

Light can be nervous, intricate, filigreed, lemony, zen, fizzy, frenetic, bold, weak, soothing and light can be

open.

POETRY IS

– after Emilio Villa

Poetry is an inexhaustible deep song dream, that pale, that dark.
Poetry is the colour of waiting for a letter
        is the colour of the bird's wing over the water in reflection
        is the colour of falling into a sober pool with your clothes on.

Poetry is a bowl
      a nest
      a yes
      a cupped hand.

Poetry is astir with silence
      with serenity.

Poetry is Lorine Niedeker's condensery
      is a wild expanse of the heart.

Poetry is a hidden hunger, an offering,
        bedraggled, filled with light, holy.
Poetry melts in your mouth not in your hands.
Poetry is a sly smile and knowing gesture.
Poetry is deeply generous, and quietly ravenous.

Poetry is dashed off
      a crashing bore
      a crushing chore
      a balm to the hoards.

Poetry is the place you set your keys down and forget where they are.
Poetry is walking into the cool barn so that the bats become unsettled,
tangling in your hair.
Poetry is a stabbing pain in the inarticulate.

Poetry is Goethe's do not hurry; do not rest.
Poetry is the tall woman you observe drinking a blood orange martini in the corner of the party, who walks away at the next approach.
Poetry is a game that is not a game. Poetry is game. Poetry tries, tries harder than the essay. Poetry continues on with or without you.
Poetry is a resistance, won't be defined by one person.
Poetry is a continuance.

Poetry is a nuanced polishing of the tiger's lustre.

MY FAVORITE

- after "My Favorite Kingdom" by Li-Young Lee

My favorite colour is
weathered turquoise on a grey and moody day.

My favorite magic trick is when silk scarves fly
into doves.

My favorite time of day is morning on a weekday when
I don't have to go to work and the suburbs
are quiet and empty thank god.

My favorite ice cream is Neapolitan though I don't remember
when I last had any because
I usually end up having green tea or pistachio flavored
sometimes coconut.
The truth is I hardly ever have ice cream.

My favorite lie is love of all kinds.

My favorite fairy tale is the one where the brothers are turned
into swans
and I have to knit sweaters for them all but of course
I don't quite finish.

My favorite scene from a movie I haven't seen in its entirety
is from La Ballon Rouge, 1956.

My favorite door is the portal when I close my eyes and walk through
into dreaming.

My favorite dreaming tells me what path to take or more often
to set out.

SEVEN REMEMBERED STILL LIFES

- after Joe Brainard's "Ten Imaginary Still Lifes"

Remembered Still Life No. 1

I close my eyes. I remember light pink peonies in smudgy sea blue vases on an outdoor table. Sheer abundance of flowers. Glasses of cold white wine. Blue cheese and figs. Dappled light from the trees. The night moves on from this moment, and we sit until the sun goes down, reluctantly leaving to go home.

Remembered Still Life No. 2

I close my eyes. I remember all the Buddhas. Earlier this summer I collected them, strangely compelled to see how many and how they would interact with each other spatially and spiritually. One from outside. I gave him a bath in the kitchen sink to get rid of spider webs and the dirt that collected in the folds of his garment. The metal one. The one that holds the pink lotus candle in a clear glass. The one my friend's young son dove or fell onto and broke the finger. The boy will likely always have a scar on his right temple. The roses had all come out and, when I was walking the dog, I borrowed a few from city property to augment my own collection. Cotton candy pink, orange and fuchsia all on the turquoise table. I don't know why I suddenly needed to arrange the Buddhas but it felt relaxing.

Still Life No. 3

I remember collecting the pieces that one day and it's stayed the same ever since. Some of the vases, the ones that look like they fell out of a Morandi painting, were from Winners. Some we took from Rob's collection in the basement. A friend brought me a metal cuff from her time in Gabon and it matches the shapes of some of the vases especially the tall handmade one, cream coloured. They all live on the library table in our front room. Mostly we dust around them, but sometimes they are all removed and then put back on the table again. But mostly in the same arrangement.

Still Life No. 4

The first still life Rob painted was in my bachelor apartment. Not long after I moved out they tore the building down, but it had its charms. A big window with a broad sill, for example, in front of which I placed my round, white table from Ikea. There were tulips on the table. A bowl of fresh strawberries, toast, jam, coffee in white cups with a blue Chinese design. I set the Pentax MX out, loaded with a new roll of film for him to find when he woke up. The painting hangs in the Canadian Embassy in Beijing.

Still Life No. 5

Our lives together have been a succession of still lifes, of noticing them. Let me tell you, they're everywhere. Beside my notebook is a diet cherry cola over ice in a clear glass, sweating in the heat. The empty can is beside it. I read the nutrition facts. A bunch of zeros. The barcode is never aesthetically pleasing. Beside them, the Nikon D80, with the lens I use on it. The one that blurs things when you get close. 50mm/1.4.

Still Life No. 6

The empty stone bowl. Today it's empty. We've owned this bowl for approximately 20 years. Sometimes it's empty and sometimes it's full.

Still Life No. 7

Joe Brainard wrote ten, but today I only want to write seven. Instead, let's talk about the endless configurations of objects that can be arranged on a visual plane. You can imagine objects, or remember them, or just look around the room where you're reading this exercise. Still lifes continue to be used by art students as an exercise in painting or drawing. There are endless sketches being churned out by first years depicting their pencil and eraser, or an apple beside a vase of dried flowers. I don't really like looking at those types of exercises because they are void of the narrative, the humming, throbbing energy that surrounds and permeates a real still life. Often when a writer describes a still life they're attempting to create a fixed point for memory. Maybe you can remember what your grandmother had on her coffee table or on the dresser in her bedroom, but you don't remember anything about the conversations that took place in those rooms. Also in novels, say, a still life that is described can act like a dream. The writer is resigned to the fact the reader needs a rest and expects half of the people will mainly glaze over skimming the passage. Certain words, though, enter the reader's consciousness. Orange, spoon, white cup, pink carnation. Pictures are formed. Sink into a person, melt, like spring snow on your plum lips.

WITH

- after Evie Shockley's poem "canvas and mirror"

Self-portrait with obscure and poetic novels, with dragonfly paperweight,
with breeze ruffling through the pages. Self-portrait with ridiculously
white eyelashes and eyebrows, with a pale visage. Self-portrait with

black dog, with morning dew, with rose bushes whose flowers change
from apricot to pink
as they bloom. Self-portrait with moments of inner calm balanced with
sad nervousness

with five year plan, less than four to go. Self-portrait with a sharp eye out
for beauty for bliss. Self-Portrait with cold white wine in the late
afternoon, with a postcard of Vermeer's girl with the red hat purchased
in the NGA gift shop. Self-portrait with a glance

over my shoulder, with mismatched eyes, with eyeglasses that seem
always like wearing a disguise. Self-portrait with diet Coke and iMac.
Self-portrait with product placement, with

hope and sometimes head scratching until it bleeds despair, with my
work published and some of it not so much, with dreams hovering
around me, with bicycle like the ones in a Remedios Varo painting. Self-
portrait with a peanut butter sandwich as a nod to Gwendolyn MacEwen.
Self-portrait with

a suitcase full of silk scarves, with tall grey boots, with long hair, with an
eye to the light, with a disappearing act.

TO A YOUNG POET

If I were to write anything resembling advice to a young poet, I'd begin by defining poet, which would be copied from Hélène Cixous – "I call "poet" any writer, philosopher, author of plays, dreamer, producer of dreams, who uses life as a time of "approaching.""

I would say a poet is anyone who has ever had the dream that the book they are writing is a desk and all night long they pull out drawers from which canter, fly, swim magical creatures. A poet will be careful what she wishes for, especially in a poem. A poet will follow Louise Glück's advice and if wishing on a butterfly, will wish for another poem.

I would go on to say that when I say young, I mean new, I mean the tender and magnificent stage of anyone of any age who is beginning to write.

I would say, read the poem by Mahmoud Darwish instead of this one. Read it for the line:

"From now on, your only guardian is a neglected future."

Read it for the line:

"The poem is always incomplete, the butterflies make it whole."

A poet should make a break for it when anyone is handing out advice. A young poet should both hear and not hear any praise they may happen to be given.

A young poet will constantly try to figure out what a poet is and what a poem might be.

A poet holds.
A poet holds down two or three jobs
A poet holds your hand.

A poet holds out.
A poet holds her head above water.
A poet is waving not drowning.

I would advise you to read Marina Abramovic's manifesto. Under "A list of an artist's friends" she writes: "An artist should have friends who lift his spirit."

I would advise you to write your own manifesto, once a year. Let your friends read it.

I would advise you not to complain when you've been given what you asked for. Anonymity for example. Solitude. Alone.

I advise you to ignore most of the advice you'll be given. To stop writing villanelles and sestinas. I advise you to spend as little time possible on the internet attempting to decipher whether a person has 'liked' something wholeheartedly, ironically, or with what degree of fatigue.

I advise you to find a nice place to write. In the mornings, a spot where you can hear the birds sing. A clearing in the woods, or on a nice park bench. In the winter, try to write your poems by a window.

Try and find a chaise longue. I'm adamant about this point. If it's threadbare, throw a blanket over it.

Learn as many languages as you are able. Obtain a card from the library of butterflies.

In the summer learn to speak: rose, pollen, dragonfly, bird nest, wing, grass – each blade a different dialect.

In winter learn to speak: frost, snow, sparkle, drift, silence.

In both seasons: play, light, dream, ennui, falling (petals or snow).

I would advise you to comb your hair before leaving the house.

Write a poem titled, "Self-Portrait" from time to time.

Breathe, and look, and wander. Sit. Enjoy the waiting. Some days radiance. Others, a dim trace, a dazzling bleakness, a dark unstylish agony.

Eventually it will be your turn to write to the young poets, from your very own neglected future. Part of you will want to tell the young poets to find something else to do, something useful. To flee from the enchantment of the book of anguish.

But if you have found some beauty and comfort in the solitude of poetry and in the marvelous futility of choreographing butterflies, then who are you to dissuade them?

IT MUST HAVE
BEEN WEIRD

IT MUST HAVE BEEN WEIRD

Where does one begin in talking about the long conversation, as it's called, between the sister arts, poetry and painting?

With Simonides' line, "painting is silent poetry, and poetry painting that speaks," or how about skipping ahead on the timeline to the 3rd Earl of Shaftesbury and his remarks about the parallels and comparisons made between painting and poetry. "Almost ever absurd and at best constrained, lame and defective." The conversation is not always tidy or lovely but often breaks out into competition, antagonism, misunderstanding, hostilities, a bit of pooh-poohing. Somewhere along the timeline of the long conversation, there are books with etchings of paintings tipped in, and then photography is invented and precious photographs of paintings, however murky, are tipped in. It's quite a miracle – the tipped in photo.

Skip ahead to the internet, to Google images, to the masses of reproductions sized and tiled and flowing, streaming, ghosting. The rapidity, the rows and rows, the pouring frothing unfixed unmediated uncurated backlit unstable forest.

How to interject in this long conversation when one grew up in a small town, then on an acreage, and now lives in the suburbs, not incidentally at latitude 53, far away from the hub of the art scene.

Ekphrasis is the vivid verbal representation of visual art. Long before the internet, poets wanted to describe, to share, something they'd seen, a painting or work of art in its absence, beginning with Homer and the shield of Achilles. I graduated from university in 1995 and I knew I wanted to write about art. I'd just married an artist, we'd been to Italy for 5 weeks on a honeymoon, looking at art every day.

What I want to say about my life until then was that I knew nothing about art. I grew up without seeing any art whatever. In grade 12, 1984, my art teacher seemed astounded by a drawing I made in the first class. She asked me if I'd heard of Joan Miró. I hadn't. She kept asking me if I was sure. I was very sure. At the end of that term we were introduced to painting. I copied a photograph from a magazine of a mountain with a lake in front. There was a red canoe in the water with a man rowing. The scene I accomplished in a satisfactory manner but the man in the canoe was difficult. I painted the canoe and the man over and over until the area in the painting was quite built up, quite thick, where the rest of the surface was thinly painted, at times only a wash. I should have left it like that, a big blob of a painted figure, but in the end I scraped it off and painted lake water over top. The red mark was still visible though and appeared as a mysterious capsized object. That summer I used the remainder of the paint I had to paint a large picture of a Big Mac that I copied from an image on the tray liner at McDonald's. I'd never heard of pop art or seen a sculpture by Claes Oldenberg or heard of Andy Warhol.

How do we see? That's a small question that's interested me ever since I can remember. And it gets more and more complicated all the time. John Berger published the groundbreaking book *Ways of Seeing* in 1972. He examined the male gaze in the context of the history of art, and famously said, "Men look at women. Women watch themselves being looked at." About twenty years later, about the time I was graduating with a B.A. in English, W.J.T. Mitchell published a book called *Picture Theory*. He says, "…in what is characterized as an age of 'spectacle,' 'surveillance,' and all pervasive image-making, we still do not know exactly what pictures are, what their relationship to language is, how they operate on observers and on the world, how their history is to be understood, and what is to be done with or about them."

I felt uneasy the whole time I wrote my first book of poems. I was interested in skirting that classical ekphrastic moment, the pure description. I was interested in subverting the male gaze, I was interested in giving voice to the marginalized, the objectified and the overlooked. I was trying to figure out what to do with these images, these pictures, that mostly I was discovering in reproduction. I bought an alumni library card and carted home huge stacks of art books.

Mainly I spent a lot of time feeling quite fraudulent, writing about paintings or artists whose work I'd only seen in reproduction. These feelings of being a fake led me to open my first book with a poem about an art forger, which later inspired a novel – *Hive: A Forgery*. Some of the paintings I wrote about I at least saw afterwards. Which eased my anxiety. I was anxious but I was also enthusiastic, curious, filled with awe, delight, and also brimming with questions. The more I looked, the more questions I had. It was a mode of learning. Looking, questioning, writing.

Would I have felt better about writing about art in reproduction if I looked at paintings inch by inch, maybe seeing detail that I wouldn't be able to glean if I was actually in front of the painting. The Metropolitan Musuem of Art's website *now* has such a tool, which would also be very useful if you had seen the painting but wanted to check to see if you'd remembered it correctly.

But ekphrasis is originally about describing a seen work of art, to someone who has no access to seeing same. Shortly after I wrote my book, the internet took off. Anyone can look up an image of almost any work of art, certainly any work of art in a museum. So you'd think that ekphrasis would be redundant, null and void. But in so many ways, I think it's just begun. Of course it hasn't been just about description – there are many subgroups of ekphrasis, many strategies taken up by poets who want to take part in the conversation about art. For example, there is the envoicing of the subject, praise poems, notional ekphrasis – where the painting or work of art is an invented one.

Does the internet make it harder for us to focus on paintings? How does looking at reproductions of paintings in different resolutions, on different scales, in changing contexts and on screens that may alter the colour, brightness, and tonal range of an image, how does this affect how we then look at a particular painting in person, or paintings in general? How does this affect our attention span?

When my daughter and I go to a museum with Rob, my partner who is an artist, his attention span is greater than ours. He is scrutinizing brushstrokes, and looking at the blending of colours, how an artist might create the illusion of shadow and light, and other points of technique. He is looking at the mud and goop and buttery, creamy muck of the paint itself. He can tell you which paintings have bristles from the artist's brush embedded in them. He looks at a painting up close, and he also looks at it from a distance, taking in the composition, the subject. Other people have looked at the entire floor of paintings while he looks at one. And we have learned to do the same, if for shorter spans of time.

In grade three my teacher noticed that I was squinting a lot. I'd probably squinted all through grade 2 as well, but no one had seen my difficulty with seeing. At the optometrist's I thought he was giving me a test and I was trying hard not to fail. *Which is better one or two?* Better? *Okay, which one is clearer?* Define clearer.

Andy Warhol said: "I always think about what it means to wear eyeglasses. When you get used to glasses you don't know how far you could really see. I think about all the people before eyeglasses were invented. It must have been weird because everyone was seeing in different ways according to how bad their eyes were. Now, eyeglasses standardize everyone's vision to 20-20. That's an example of everyone becoming more alike. Everyone could be seeing at different levels if it weren't for glasses."

I think it must have been weird. But I think it's still weird, how we see things. What we focus on and what we miss. Remember when it was discovered that advertisers were putting subliminal messages in the images in their ads? The glass filled with gin and ice cubes? And hidden in the cubes, you could make out the word SEX? What a shocking revelation that was at the time. I'm interested in what sorts of things are hidden in the images and advertisements that we see flash by our eyes on Facebook or as we Google images and sift through them on the internet.

But mostly I'm interested in all the many ways we see paintings. There's the museum or gallery experience, seeing things at a walking speed, or out of the corner of one's eye, or for various lengths of time. How do people experience art in their own homes? The light changes throughout a day, we look at a painting in various moods – happiness, sadness. We grow older, we look at other people looking at the paintings we hang in our houses. How do we see ourselves, looking at paintings?

Even though our vision is most often standardized to 20-20, how do we as sometimes exhausted and frayed and joyful human beings see the same things differently from each other, and how do we remember, internalize and blossom into images?

In 1912 Monet was diagnosed with cataracts in both eyes. A couple of years later he said, "I no longer saw colours with the same intensity. The reds seemed muddy to me, the pinks insipid and the intermediate colours and lower tones escaped me completely." When I sift through images on the computer they are so filled with light that prolonged looking burns my eyes. The reds are too bright and the pinks are too candy flossed. I know there are tones that are escaping me completely. But the fact is I can, for example, see images that I would not otherwise have access to. I can look at all of Vermeer's thirty-four paintings lined up on one webpage, and I can also look at them in scale to one another – not usually possible in real life.

What does it mean to want to translate images into words? Even as its phantom stares at you out of the computer screen? In this process of translation, how do the materials of painting permeate the materials of writing? How do we see when we close our eyes? How do we remember and mis-remember what we have seen and are we any closer to knowing how pictures and texts interact with each other and how they operate on observers?

I guess what is most interesting to me (and I think it's the constant in the conversation between painting and poetry) is that *very moment of seeing* and the desire to suture the skin of seeing, that moment, that image, wherever it's been seen, to a string of words, to text.

CONVENTIONS
of
EKPHRASIS

THINGS THAT RUN THROUGH MY HEAD WHEN WRITING AN EKPHRASTIC POEM

My approach is in spirals, I walk around in my mind, around the painting. I try to see the supports, the stretcher and the nails, the frame might be important. It might not be. The tooth of the canvas is of particular interest of course.

Ecstatic, elastic, there is often a fragrance that must be absorbed.

I think about the word, ekphrastic. A cough. A quiver, a thrum. A clearing of the throat. I think about tomato soup being poured whole out of a can, adding milk to it. That glory.

I think about ekphrasis as a rhetorical device, how I'm too old for rhetorical devices, and how I'm afraid of heights. And I won't even get into the competition aspect of the procedure. More than anything else I crave an inner peace and a solitude. Sometimes what I really want to write about is exhaustion and shyness which might make matters not worse exactly, but I think it would make me less sympathetic to the spectrum of ineluctable encounters with suburbanites.

Sure I have all the usual sumptuously banal anxieties that anyone writing an ekphrastic poem would have. Embarrassment in advance at the failure of language. There are Beckett lines that arrive unbeckoned. Try again. I can't go on. Unbeckoned Beckett.

I try to slow it all down at first. Slow down the words, the lines. They start to ricochet off one another at a certain point. Pop Rocks in my mouth. If I need a break I put a menthos candy into a bottle of Coca-Cola.

I don't mean to brag but when I wrote my first book, hardly anyone was talking about ekphrasis or knew what it meant. I was constantly defining it, talking about how I had attempted to skirt the ekphrastic moment. Subsequently some people said some nice things about books I wrote, and some people said some not so nice things. And once I was compared to one of the characters in the Charlie's Angels movie. Unrelatedly, you could suppose, there was a long time during which I couldn't write poetry at all, the muse, who looked a bit like one of Charlie's original TV series Angels in my mind, left. This happens, poetry abandons a poet, sometimes forever. I remember reading about how Roo Borson gives up poetry, twice, how it returns to her. When it first happened to me I didn't quite believe poetry had really and truly packed her red Samsonite suitcase and left.

It's possible to think of ekphrasis as an embellishment, a challenge, an interference. But also a type of thievery or forgery. A case could be made for ekphrasis as dreamish rigor. As a flying too close to the sun with waxen wings.

Ekphrasis can be charming, a connoisseurship of flattery. Of flattening. There is a fluidity, at times mockery.

I calm my qualms, agree with my greed, the deception of my descriptions. I evade, disguise. Shimmering deferrals mirage with a nervous noise. There is an inundation of ornament in this process that turns silence into vixened words. The alembic umbilical usurps the syrup.

It's complicated, maybe more complicated than you might read in W.J.T. Mitchell's *Picture Theory*. It's certainly one correct possibility, he gets at the heart of it, laying out the struggle – indifference/hope/fear.

I make excuses, it's such a false process, I can't. The tranquility of the syntax, the secret indecorous synonyms, draw me back toward them. We don't need to turn paintings into poems any more you know, there's the internet, Google images. Brueghel's *Fall of Icarus*, you can look that up. If you do you might find Auden's poem and this line which is not in the poem: "In so far as poetry, or any of the arts, can be said to have an ulterior purpose, it is, by telling the truth, to disenchant and disintoxicate."

So I've had that wrong all along, too. Believing in intoxication and enchantment. Unraveling a certain spatial ravishment. Imbrications of types of beauty. I will swagger anyway with Baudelaire, and call his call, "Be Drunk!" (It's the only way).

There are prophecies that must be respected, the high-handed to avoid. Pitfalls. There is the inevitable grief, the distress a curious brocade. That will ring a bell, this will. For thee.

Whatever it is you've managed to write, (and writing about anything – it's been said – is just an excuse, an excuse to say what you wanted to say but couldn't, not so openly as all that) will be diminished, a diminishment. Textureless. A purgatory, an impatient in-between. Flawed. Problematic. At best, an incandescent glance open to misinterpretation and accusations – hysterical, fancy, beyond your reach, disconnected.

In the end it's pleasant to think about studio exercises, about the long and steady practice of an art form through a life, about conventions of politeness and the expectations and obligations of inspiration. I'm clearing my throat now, I'm looking forward with curiosity and an openness of spirit.

PAINTING OF WOMAN SITTING IN A MUSEUM WRITING (NOTIONAL)

Still. She sits, she stations herself. First in a hum a milling crowd. Before she had stood. This distance. That. Stood in the corner off to the side. Left. Returned. Is transfixed. Now sits elbow on crossed knee, back curved. Encounters, recognizes, hears hidden echoes. On the chestnut leather bench. Medium Firm. Posture. She thinks about her posture. Back not so straight as she'd like. Squints. Thinks wrinkles, crows' feet, blinks, smooths. Alone now. Docent vacates. Can see a sleeve, a leaning against the threshold. Feels harmless, assessed. Thinks about wombs ports dominions. She raises her arm slightly. Strokes air alone, daub dab swish. Filled brimming with honeysuckled ekphrastic hope ecstatic. Secretly she had wished, wishes, she could paint. That she could merge with colour, Venetian pink, alizarin crimson, turmeric, common madder, verdigris. Takes out small leather bound notebook. Pencil point on paper. Rests. She gazes. Raises an eyebrow. Discerns, is ironic, melts, quavers, envies. Is pulled. She wonders what the painter kept, held back. The painting the paint the colours the brushstrokes – in turn violent and soothing and incomprehensible wild – the image enters her skin. Speaks to her. Begins a mute quarrel. She resists holds back she engages responds soaks up sensuously she understands. Shudders sparks breathless bliss. Closes her eyes, leans back, lips apart, listens, feels the sparks, the rhythms of intimate gestures. No, yes, now, leans in drowns in a din of colour, delightedly smitten, chosen to receive, to be astonished in this exact way. She is conscious, tranquil, she ponders the symptoms of Stendhal's syndrome. Remembers Achille's shield, remembers destiny, sincere trembling. Thinks about the unutterable order of things, their eloquent circuitry, of picture theories, of shift and turn, of representin', of representation, of suturing text and image. The quarrel becomes louder, tense, she meets it she praises lingers languishes in deception juxtaposition translation replication. She gives and gives. She distorts, desires, invents. Battles struggles. What are limitations? Verklempt, she envoices, ventriloquizes gives voice.

Critiques flatters falters is afraid. She fears collapse. Overcomes. Wades into illusion quill to lip. Truth? Reality? Souls revealed? She battens flattens returns to battle to antagonism she speaks to, speaks from, knows secrets knows silence embraces limitations enters the gap the convex mirror the rabbit hole the old duck-rabbit conundrum, hears vases talk, jars talk, pipes disclaim. Phantoms the gap between language and image. Is ambivalent. Has failed. Aesthetically. She sits in the site of minor yet glorious aesthetic failure. Wind knocked out of her. Deflated where before she had been elated. Ekphrasis as fraudulence, full knowledge of that, sunk, drowning, shuddering. She sits a sham without words beyond words pretty as a picture. Waits, hope, a lesser hope returns. She sits with beauty with truth with eye of the beholder, she's been operated upon by images, been under surveillance, been invisible, just yesterday she bought the latest shade of lipstick. But now she sees an excess an interarticulated impatient moment. She collects unravelments excess with butterfly nets, looks over her shoulder. Fight gone out of her replaced with questions theories possibilities sensations interpretations conversions reconfigurations captivations awe. Stands. Takes one last sturdy look around the room, drinks of it, closes her notebook, takes it with her.

ATTUNED (THE MUSEUM GUARD SPEAKS)

Voices coming from the device on her belt reminds me of an unrecovered flight recorder or black box because the sounds will never be replayed and it makes me think of loved ones left behind.

People talk in low tones before paintings. A woman reaches over and leans against a man, her chin on his shoulder, her hand in his back pocket. She murmurs.

A mother talks to her teenaged daughter and both of them are nodding. The mother drapes her arm briefly over the daughter's shoulder but withdraws it comfortably in a short time and one can see that there has been a concession on either side, an understanding of each other's requirements.

A man is drawn to a painting and realizes how close he is and moves back and circles away, but then returns. He looks over his shoulder at the guard who is looking at him. Eyes connect. They are both determinedly expressionless.

When a poet takes on the voice of the guard, what is happening? As that poet, I am a mix of envy and worry because she gets to spend so much time with a painting I love but also that if she sees it every day it might become invisible or difficult to see. I concede that she knows more about the painting than I ever will.

In a room full of people engaged in acts of persistent concentration, inarticulate observation, and awed, blessed mutterings coinciding with the at times luminous solitudes that a work of art possesses or the defiant escape into colour that they represent, the guard is often the last thing you might notice, if you notice at all.

Vigilance as a calling is represented as an aloof vulnerability in someone who also is attuned to the skin of painting simultaneous with the possibility of attack. Concealed pocket knifes, cans of spray paint, tubes of lipstick, these are the obvious. Verbal abuse, the cold shoulder, the brief dismissal, these too, call for attentiveness.

But surely we can imagine more. A particular affinity for a neglected painting. Roast beef dinner after a long shift on the weekend. University degrees, books absorbed. Let's recognize boredom, sore feet, disgust, elation and joy. Let us admit, merely, she is a bird in the storm of art.

WHAT WE SEE NEVER RESIDES (RESPONSE TO ANOTHER POET'S EKPHRASIS)

When I read about the space between poetry and painting, about that gap, my eye often joins the two words gap and space, and then makes sense of that by turning it into: *grace*. So then I'm thinking about the grace of that break, the scuffed and hope filled chasm, between poetry and painting, which might just mean I'm due for an appointment with the optometrist.

"It is in vain that we say what we see; what we see never resides in what we say," according to Michel Foucault. Ekphrastic poems run the risk of being a lot more amusing to write than to read, much the same as it's more fun to play tennis than to watch it on TV. So I assume, since I neither play nor watch. But I do have this insane faith that once in a while what we see does seep into what we say or maybe it doesn't reside in the words, but above or beside or in the breath we use to speak the words.

I've listened in on conversations where people, often poets, list all the Vermeers they've seen, and sometimes I've mentioned the poem by Alfred Corn titled "Seeing All the Vermeers." I don't mean to deflate people, I just think it's a very cool poem to have written, though the news of it does sort of seem to have that affect. Was it something they'd been planning to do, once they'd seen them all? Or is it because they hadn't thought of it but wish they had? Or because they'd previously thought it to be mostly an impossible thing?

As for me, I've long wanted to write a poem about Alfred Corn's poem. Which is in fact one of the modes, or conventions of ekphrasis – response to another poet's response to a work of art. But you can see why I've resisted. Not only does it sound decidedly unpoetic, but there's also this underlying sense of persnickety competition to the endeavor. *I've seen the Vermeers more intensely, written about them more exquisitely than you.* Which is a stance I really do try to refrain from. I mean, let's. You know?

But then I start to count them up, go over the ones I've seen, the museums where we've seen them, and it's comforting. The National Gallery in London, The Louvre, The Met, The Frick, The Rijksmuseum, Mauritshuis. Seventeen of the thirty-seven. Which begins to sound like bragging, even though it's really a sort of yearning. Because they get away from me. And I want to remember what it was like standing in front of *The Lacemaker* in Paris, or *The Milkmaid* in Amsterdam, or *Study of a Young Woman* in New York, all these light-filled women, the way they lean effortless into the mysterious vibrations of light so it finds them, just so.

I could list the ones I darkly pine for, long to see. *Woman Holding a Balance, Girl with a Red Hat, Woman with a Pearl Necklace.* Talk about that kind of yearning, and how it differs from the yearning to see what has been seen.

What I'm most interested in is this use Corn makes of the poem as a vessel for remembrance, as a way of seeing again. In taking stock, rather lovingly, of where and in what circumstances he's looked at the Vermeers, he also lets his readers experience how beauty has imprinted itself on him through time, how it is possible to measure ourselves against a certain kind of gathering, of strands of light, glory, illuminations, silence and a precise joy in colour. And yes, the grace of that measuring.

HAY-COLOURED WINGS (ENARGIA)

- from the Greek, meaning to make visible, lively, palpable before the reader's eye.

I don't want to forget how fine it is to write quietly, alone, in the soft clarity of winter light. Winter quiet is so lovely that I sometimes believe I prefer it to summer quiet and that deep, soul melting light. Maybe I already do for I wouldn't at present trade this for a summer day. I take my books and journals upstairs to write as I sit on the chaise longue in my bedroom window. In a rare moment of poetic intoxication, I write that I will not leave until I jot down something that aches and throbs and flutters and flits. That's how alive it is.

I become fixated on the paper thinness of the clouded sky out the window, and then how the faint light eases onto the bright white paper, suffusing it with a wooly grey warmth. The light a kind of spirit. I think of the butterflies in 17th century Dutch paintings, part flower, part stained glass window. How blithely and with what gentleness and dignity they exist, these painted hinges, these doors leading us into the dream of flight. For if we haven't the power to imagine ourselves in flight like a swallow or bright cardinal, then perhaps the marmalade butterfly's path with its secret and exalted correspondence with flowers is easier to dream.

I think there are details of paintings that want to be brought to life, into dreams, on their own. We slip through the painting via these moments and alight. And they bear our weight, our existences, us.

I wish to write about a single painted butterfly so that it flies before you, and one day you will see that painting and know it as the one I'm talking about. But I don't have that sort of confidence any more in my ability to describe things and I wonder what it was like to have to summon all one's powers when there was no television or internet or giant billboards or glossy art magazines.

When my daughter was small, I remember closing my eye against her cheek, batting my pale eye lashes, and telling her, butterflies, and then she would do the same to me. When I tucked her into bed she would sometimes request butterflies. How soft her freckled cheek was, how strong the grip of her small hands around my neck.

Dreams and memories fly and flutter within us, inexhaustible, and at times it seems wise to keep them secret in your mind rather than chasing them with a net and glass jar, showing them to just anyone.

Still, I would like to write about my butterfly but now I find that when you Google *enargia*, it is also a term that refers to a sort of moth. Which leads me to think of Virginia Woolf's *The Death of the Moth*, its hay-colored wings, and how it possesses, in spite of its drabness, the very energy of the world. Such a force at the end of a small life, dancing. In the 14th century Hafiz wrote, "Be wise. Cast all your votes for Dancing!" And this is how it is, you must cast your votes for the fragility of words and butterflies and other winged creatures. It's all we can do, to see, and to try and make the seen visible, palpable.

7 REECE MEWS, SOUTH KENSINGTON (ARTIST'S STUDIO)

"Everything was covered with a fine orange and pink dust," said John Edwards, Francis Bacon's friend. Flower pollen of the soul, is the first thing that comes to mind, and the dust, orange and pink, sinks into me like a soft scream into a pillow belonging to someone else.

It took archaeologists three years to catalogue over 7500 items, dismantle and reassemble the studio in Dublin and now you can peek into the mess and chaos from three vantage points.

Every artist's studio has a little something in common with the Bacon studio. Whether it's paint that's dribbled over the edge of the table where the palette resides, or a myriad of brushes in jars and tin cans. Tubes of paint, rolled up, squeezed to get the last bit out. Magazine clippings. Towers of art books. Slashed canvases. But this studio seems to contain all studios, it's the studio you fall backward into in dreams of metamorphoses preceded by a ruffling of colours like the rainbowed wings in a Fra Angelico annunciation painting.

The more I look at photographs of the studio, the cleaner my own house seems, the cleaner the studio in my own basement, but also, my thoughts become cluttered and I start to feel panicked and begin ordering the objects on my desk in ways similar to Saul Steinberg's drawing of a table and its contents.

In Bacon's studio: layers of paint tubes, brushes, turpentine, boxes and boxes filled with photos, clippings. The book on Seurat covered in dots of paint. He used ripped up corduroy trousers and old socks to daub at his paintings, to lay things on thick and to texture. The door used as a palette, the wall too. Nowhere an actual palette. Masses of stretchers faced toward the wall. A bust. Dried paint. Cases of wine, some full, some empty. Photos and clippings from magazines of open mouths, people mid-scream, yawning, singing, calling out, gobsmacked. A plaid hat, a fan, a radio, splattered mirror, old shoes, newspapers. Layers and layers. The bathtub in the kitchen. His bed in another room where you can see the floor. Pink bedspread, orange pillowcases. A chartreuse velvet couch.

Everything covered in a fine orange and pink dust. Quietly. The dust of all those screams. The depths of everything we abandon in ourselves and others and the rigors of the chaos we contain for short intervals.

It's too easy to say that this nest of clutter which he said enabled him to paint properly, was a reflection of what he was trying to create on the canvases, or what was going on in his mind.

A thick, woven history of his place in time. Leaving just enough space in the middle for an easel, a canvas, a location to keep the anguish out, the anguish in. Visitors, it is said, were few.

A fine orange and pink dust covered everything. It was catalogued and photographed and breathed in for three years by archaeologists and conservators.

There was a time I wanted to become a painter because I desired to paint the pink and orange wings of angels in the perceptible moment of the crossing over into the isolation of our present consideration of time, but my skills were incommensurate. I wonder how much of the pull to write about the artist's studio comes back to glimmers of envy, jealousy, or maybe just a small but tender and exposed twinge felt when experiencing the secret light of the person you weren't meant to become.

A fine orange and pink dust covers everything.

All I need to get across is that the dust is a point of envy because it's a visible sign of a life lived near the gap into the wondrous, the "crack" where, as Rilke or Leonard Cohen or Balthus might say, the light gets through. And that while the writer must frequently leave the study to practice telepathy, to walk inconsolable on wooded paths or in fields of daffodils or around some misty lake, the artist may set up camp and remain tethered to the deep mirror, to the fierceness of those vibrations.

BREATH TAKINGS (PRAISE)

Meetings, sighs, breathings. Breathtaking. Stings. Tinglings. Stinglings. A give and take, a taking in, an engagement, a falling into.

There are sparks, bliss. Pangs. Palpitations. You have marveled and deliberated and whirled and felt alive, illuminated, or you've been drawn into the commotion of a painting, into its singing. Or you've had an experience of the divine.

The painting has reminded you that you've been too long apart from the storm blossom of your soul.

You squint, your eyes widen. You leave it, return. You see it with your eyes closed. And sometimes you have a dream in which the painting hangs on your very own wall.

The stance then, the approach, must be praise.

And when you praise, you realize, it takes nothing away from you. But you don't overpraise which would spoil it. You don't gush. You don't flounce. It's not about you, not exactly. Though there is a selfish aspect to this process you know what is gained, who gains more. Your response is quiet and precise and attempts to be worthy of the object of praise. You are equal to the task. You are not equal to the task.

There is no trace of the backhanded compliment, the undercut. That's for somewhere else.

When you begin praising, the work becomes intense again. Your work becomes intense again, bright.

It may be relevant to note that there are limits, and the potential to reach that point of inarticulateness, awkwardness, perhaps because you over reached, perhaps because you felt an intimacy that hadn't been granted.

No matter. You'll have entered into the praise wholeheartedly, pure of soul. And you'll be able to keep them with you, those words of praise, that work of art, as a single remembered feeling. Isn't that what brought you to the word, *ekphrasis*? And even though you will go on to explore your distrust of certain images, the ethical repercussions of a work of art through time, the unhealthiness and futility of your envy, the inevitable agendas that will adhere to you, and other quarrels and contradictions and reservations you will be unable to avoid, eventually, you will wander back to praise.

WHAT LIGHT (COMPETITION)

It is the month of May as I write this, stealing glimpses over my computer screen to the pink-tinged apple blossoms outside my window.

In the good old days before Google and Instagram and Photoshop and Facebook and Flickr and before Android and iPhone and iPad and giant flat screen televisions, it was more or less understood that words had won that old competition. Words captured images. Controlled them. Corralled them. Were victorious. At least some of the poets accepted the company line.

Leonardo da Vinci introduced the term *paragone*, Italian for *comparison*. Naturally, his claim was for the difficulty of painting, and the 'supremacy of sight.' Fighting words, maybe.

Poets writing about art in this particular tradition had something to prove, self-serving motivations, dreams about domination, superiority complexes. They knew how to dance around a subject, how to be holier than, how to mimic, emulate, deliver an upper cut, how to volley, jockey, position, posture, impose, pose as impostor. How to expose ruses, play power politics. How to flatter while implicitly critiquing. How to bring up immutability and stasis, the temporal vs the spatial, at the dinner table. Bury feelings of envy in a cleverly quarreled argument. How to call into question a monumental work of art with a feathered phrase. How to jab, spar, swerve, duck, duke it out. They knew some fancy footwork. And how to look down their noses, how to appear learned, and what goes with tweed, how to find the cheapest cafes. How to move from blasé, from suffering, from speechless, to winner winner chicken dinner.

I won't go into W.J.T. Mitchell's stages of ekphrasis – indifference, hope, fear. I mean, the writers of ekphrasis know before they begin, it's a doomed, fraught, unnerving process. The rabbit has left the hat and is busy multiplying exponentially in other realms. In vain do we try to make it reappear, to pin it down, pin it on Pinterest. And yet, the inevitable failure seems only to egg us on.

But nowadays, when you read about the tradition of competition in ekphrasis, you hear phrases like, "the forging of alternative relationships" "rejection of the paragonal" "banding together" "collusion, commiseration, and sympathy" "mutual agency" and "possibility of exchange."

Nowadays, we concede before we begin. We navigate, negotiate, we sail into that gap between word and picture and stuff messages in bottles, questions. We might ask, what light do poems give paintings? What colours do paintings give poems? How to move from one magical realm to another? We ask, how to dwell in that peaceful dream for a spell.

PACK OF SMOKES (DESCRIPTION)

Maybe you had nothing else to write. You were young and thankfully, had yet to experience a tragedy, or had your heart dashed against the rocks. If in the beginning you were bored and looked upon this as an exercise, a way to hone your poetic skills, now you want to move closer.

There's a painting you love. You don't know why yet. The curve of smudgy grapes. The way the old boots seem to be made of mud. The feather in a hat and the light on hands holding cards.

Is it love, or is it a sort of hunger, that spurs you on? You want to see and see again. "Description is made both more moving and more exact when it is acknowledged that it is inevitably incomplete," says Mark Doty.

Is it the beauty of the painting, an earthenware jug made with a minimum of brushstrokes, the way the buttons on a dress are gestured toward, that compels you? Is it the texture of the paint, or the skill of the painter? Have you been pulled, gasping, into a scene so completely that you wish to understand why?

The work of art has been forged in secret, and now you, too, enter into that secrecy.

It should be simple. She leans over to place the bread on the cabinet. In her right hand a white bag with a butchered lamb's feet protruding. (You only know it's a lamb because you read it on the internet). The dish on the floor, the bottles nearby – one upturned – become more mysterious with looking. The model – who was she? You read that the same model appears in other paintings by Chardin. You only want to describe, but you're drawn into the story of the painting – the popularity of the image, the multiple renderings, the engravings. You begin to compare it to other paintings of servants by other artists. Is she eavesdropping? You spend half the day wondering whether her expression is one of toned down amusement, or weariness, or mild surprise. Is she flushed with the effort of carrying things from the market or is there a little embarrassment, too?

"One uses colour, but one paints with feeling," said Chardin. And you get tied up in knots, in the effort to turn words into colour, into feelings. You gesture, flounder, you begin the game of trying to throw flower petals into a dish, often missing the mark entirely. You're aware, all too aware, that you're selling the painting short, you're selling yourself short. If you can't make it here, you can't make it anywhere.

It's real. It's heavy. It's quiet. The way she points her toe, in the pointed shoe. The shadow below her dress. The colour of the dress, the hint of blue underneath the grey. You come back to the bread, it's size and heft.

From here, the poet either continues or goes out to buy a pack of smokes, a liter of milk, a loaf of Wonderbread, and doesn't come back.

PROD A WOUND (VENTILOQUIZE)

{vent
trill
disguise}

Doubt will creep in. As you rummage in the tickle trunk of art history, find someone to speak for, someone to speak for you.

The painting speaks. From a museum wall. Or propped, facing the wall, behind a door. This idea that a painting could see, and not just be an object to be seen.

Or a figure in the painting speaks, this is the more usual approach.

To revise, hypnotize, be hypnotized, inhabit the historical, imagine it. Re-envision, re-vision. Reveal. And in revealing, say something about yourself.

Soliloquize. Put on airs. Understand. Understudy. Practice method acting.

There are pros and cons. Qualms.

The game is absurd but also freeing, allows you to become eloquent, angry, blissful, beleaguered, weary, powerful.

The process. Creepy. Fraught. Instructive.

Putting words in painted mouths, walking a mile in someone else's shoes, seeing through eyes not your own.

Appropriation, approximation.

How will you research for your role? Tend bar? Wear a corset? Lie naked on the grass? Walk through a field of sunflowers? Drink absinthe? Wear a plumed hat? Sit? And sit some more? Look out windows? Hold a parasol? Herd cattle? Read a book? Hold a candle? Pour milk? Write a letter? Wield a sword? Play cards? Blow bubbles? Prod a wound? Tempt fate? Play a lyre?

Make annunciations?

SAINT CATHERINE OF ALEXANDRIA, BY PIETRO LORENZETTI, 1342 (SEEING YOURSELF IN A PAINTING)

Only afterwards do you realize you look nothing like her but this has zilch to do with the sensation of losing yourself and then wishing you could replicate the conditions for such an encounter with the ease with which this occurs on holodecks in science fiction television.

I'd never seen the painting before in reproduction and had no foreknowledge or premonition of the encounter.

I walked up to her with my eyes busy, aslant on other objects, and even at times the floor.

When you run into someone from your past at the mall while doing your Christmas shopping and your hands are full of packages and they come at you sidelong. You start talking to them before you know who they are even though they spotted you from a distance and use your name in a greeting. Incrementally, the recognition sinks in and while you continue talking you congratulate yourself for not giving away the fact you had not a blessed clue who they were for several minutes.

There was the moment of merging, a pleasant feeling of dreamy unearthly melting into a golden reflection without questioning why there would be a mirror hanging in the Metropolitan Museum of Art, a confusion of the senses, the smell of orange blossoms. Who was I?

The pleasure of such an encounter is analyzed at a later date. The energy from the collision fuels the dream of examining a painting from the inside, an empathic connection, rather than from an oppositional stance. Coming into her presence unanticipated and completely unaware yet magnetized was a delight akin to being absorbed into the infinitely quiet fireworks of a sunset, melting orange and raspberry sorbet.

After the spell of merging, a kind of molting of the self, there is the downy shock of separation, a voice like a transmission at closing time, saying, *shake it off,* as though you'd received a blow in the ring, floating like a butterfly, you've been stung by a bee.

The mystery of the painting has to do with how the artist embedded a mirror just below the thin skin of paint.

I was in the midst of coming out of this delirium when my daughter, then ten years old, walked up behind me and said, she looks just like you. Except for the crown.

I look nothing like her. Her eyes are chestnut and mine are mismatched, blue and green. Her nose is thin. But we have similar small lips, similar complexion. We both have blonde hair.

This brief connection, moment of astonishment, reminds me how tricky it is to see oneself. You are yourself a mystery, catching only slender traces, extraordinary shadows. The light shining behind you from a closet door eclipsing your reflection in a handheld mirror reads as true. One day, you're a colourful blur in a store window. But sometimes, in a painting. Exposure. A sliver from a hidden mirror. The chance to look at yourself and say, *I honor the divine in you.*

THINKING IN PAINT (GESTURES OF THE PAINTER)

Every artist has a private catalogue of the types of brushstrokes and techniques, even if they don't have words for them. It's confusing, you see. So many variables including the diameter of brush, and the degree to which the brush is loaded. Colour is a factor. One brushstroke may occur at several different layers of the overall surface. Length of the brushstroke is important, surface covered. Does the brushstroke indicate light or shadow or an unusual texture or a smooth one? Is it made decisively, or nervously? In a mood of happiness or despair? Wet onto dry, or wet into wet? Is it a streak or a scumble, a gouge or a feathering? Thick or thin? Viscose or muddy.

When I say it's confusing I mean that it's a splendid confusion, and who would want to leave that communion, interrupt it with words. The struggle is *with* paint rather than *against* it.

The reason students often begin by copying well known paintings is that there are ways of smearing the paint on canvas that you won't find in how-to books or manuals and maybe this is because if the artist has been *thinking in paint* for so long as to have absorbed its lessons, then breaking the silence seems something of a betrayal.

Here you might imagine that it's necessary to create a language to express how paint is handled, but painting is a language.

It takes most of a lifetime to learn how paint behaves. There are still artists struggling to understand the myriad ways to manipulate oil paint, a renaissance invention, in spite of all the possible modern and technological ways to produce art. This is not, as James Elkins says, "because they are suspicious of technology, but because there is so much to learn about even the simplest substances."

Elkins describes a student learning to copy a Monet painting. How impossible it is because of the insane variety of strokes and jabs and shapes, the angles which Monet comes at the canvas. He swirls and jabs, is rough and then gentle. His brush flies and shimmers and scratches. Attacks, caresses, glides, dabs.

When you watch a film of Pollock's 'action painting' it teaches you about the idea of making a mark on a canvas and the fact that it's a complicated thing to do, maybe increasingly so, as we move through time, ever distant from the Renaissance, as is evident in all the comments left below the YouTube video.

Some find it freeing, mystical, allowing the paint to trace their feelings and bring them into a radiance.

Pollock's process increases their compassion for what a person can do in a given set of circumstances, how it is possible to skim across surfaces and to adhere, fragmented, predestined, like the paths of stars. Others are enraged. The incensed comment by the unemployed autoworker about the three year old throwing paint is remarkably ignored, though the innocently asked question, *what is art?* - is taken up.

Still, in spite of the tension that arises when confronting the creation of a field of beauty, others will attempt to soothe. Even though I am a fan of the rigorous shadows of Goya, writes one viewer, I can appreciate that this technique tells us something about Goya's working methods in so far as it comes close to exposing the mind of a working artist.

THE COPYIST IN THE NATIONAL GALLERY, WASHINGTON, D.C.
(IN A MUSEUM)

"Painting is the most magical of mediums. The transcendence is truly amazing to me every time I go to a museum and I see how somebody figured another way to rub colored dirt on a flat surface and make space where there is no space or make you think of a life experience."
- Chuck Close

The copyist had accomplished part of the underpainting for the Dutch landscape and it complemented the muted and mottled floral pattern on her blouse. Her long khaki skirt and low pink-beige heels, and the coffee-coloured mat provided by the museum, were part of the composition, and the blue strings of her apron picked up the blue-grey tones of the underpainting which could also have been a map of an island.

As if she were a pretense for doing so, I took several photographs of her, and the guard, sweeping into and out of the room, made every effort to stay out of the frame.

Her sustained presence in the room altered the air around the paintings, opening up space where there had been no space, reminding those who strayed into the room or arrived there by more precise inclinations, that beneath the varnished surfaces of the paintings, there was paint, or as the artist Chuck Close calls it, colored dirt.

I couldn't help but wonder if she was listening to all the things that people said as they walked by, thinking maybe, like the paintings, that she couldn't hear them. However, as Edmond de Goncourt once said, "A painting in a museum hears more ridiculous opinions than anything else in the world." But I kept thinking, they must, she must, hear crazy beautiful things, too, even if she's only interested in seeing the painting she copies.

Busy looking at the paintings, still I noticed how one person would call another over because they *had* to see something, be shown. A tangible yet quiet excitement would strengthen the shimmering in the room. My seeing was influenced by witnessing a deep interest, amazement, transcendence, in those that breezed through the rooms and sometimes lingered before a particularly pleasing disturbance of a flat stretch of coloured dirt, coloured mud.

In the photograph I took, the presence of the copyist, framed by the maple doorway and shot from the room beside it, might be a manifestation of when a painting touches us and we feel luminous, and how this incomprehensibly triggers a desire to meet it through colour.

Hope fills the space around each copyist and at times this is intermingled with relief when the work which appears to be at a more advanced stage doesn't embarrass those who wander by.

Some people are magnetized and stop to stare intently at the work in progress, comparing it to the original and it's impossible to tell if those looking approve or disapprove of the liberties the copyist takes based on their skill level and comprehension of the goals of the artist.

Others walk by quickly, pretending the copyist doesn't exist in an authentic form even though they are careful not to enter the tense and worn and at times flustered or confident corridor of sight between easel and original.

If the copyist gets her version of the painting to resemble the original closely enough then most people would consider the finished painting a success at the same time as dismissing it from their view. The copy in progress is infinitely more attractive because it reminds us of the possibility of transcendence via coloured dirt rather than the possibility that the coloured dirt may just be that.

SYMPTOMS (TRANSFIXED)

The symptoms sound like something out of a fairytale or a Greek myth:

speechless, breathless, seized, ravished, spellbound, enthralled, motionless, riveted, mesmerized, enraptured, absorbed, gripped, hooked, bewitched, transfixed.

You can't ask for this but if you persist in looking for what is heart stopping, it's as inevitable as apples or gingerbread or frogs.

How long will the spell last, how long silence? Indefinite.

Words, guessed at, coaxed into the correct combination may or may not break it.

May or may not induce the same response in the reader.

COUNTING (RE-VISION)

It's the eye that is important, the I, the she, the seeing, seething, the seeing of things, the how, the visualization, eye zation, visual-I-zation.

It's the counting of vertebrae, the background check. It's not forgetting. The corpse of the prostitute dredged from the Tiber. It's feeling trapped, it's a canary in a birdcage beside her. It's a swan, glorious, overpowering. It's about being recumbent, naked, clothed, the object, about being cold. It depends on this or that. On hither and thither. It's a head on a plate, it's an olive leaf, a smile, an apple, a serpent, a dragon. It's the overlooked, the absent, the present.

It's about reading this on the National Museum of Women in the Arts website: "Only 5% of the art currently on display in U.S. museums is made by women artists."

It's about all those 19th century women depicted in terms of nature, sensuality, and domesticity.

It's still about the male gaze. It's a reminder that John Berger wrote *Ways of Seeing* in 1972. It's about the weight of things, scales, balancing, and wondering how far we've come baby.

It's about beauty and a gripping ugliness, about appreciating, about re-imagining, considering angles. It's about the birth of Venus, various hats, mirrors, scarves, corsets. It's about access, about studying, about living in the shadow. It's about servants, maids, pearls, letters, the Sabine women, various annunciations, various positions. It's about moving forward by looking back, persistence, doggedness, household names. It's about

embroidery flowers childbirth drinking tea reading books looking in the mirror picnics war animals being led to slaughter self-portraits dinner parties lost eyes and poverty and riches.

It's about

context notions intersections challenging conditions representation anger joy critical feminist discourse about feeling thinking understanding about assumptions inspiration framing and re-framing.

RAT GNAW (LIVES OF THE ARTISTS)

Of course we're drawn to them, we poets, we writers. Of course.

Vasari started it off with Cimabue, though these days, no one gets too far past the first entry to delve into the detailed whereabouts of the Renaissance artists, who their patrons were, who instructed them, and what family they married into, probably because we're too busy watching *Entertainment Tonight* to see if Jennifer Aniston has finally found Mr. Right.

But all the themes are there, misfortune, drama, Perugino's poverty spurring him to success, for example. The orphan Fra Filippo Lippi, a terrible student but exceptional at drawing, leaves the monastery to party with friends on a boat but is captured by a Moorish galley and enslaved for 18 months. He's released when he draws a brilliant likeness of the ship's master.

The stories, both believed and not. A young Giotto paints a fly on a canvas by Cimabue, which Cimabue repeatedly tries to shoo away.

"I doubt that Titian ever felt this rat gnaw," says one of the characters in Virginia Woolf's *The Waves*. It's their absorption we ever will envy. Their silence. Because after all, the work is the work, and the endless web of justification and the staking out of territory is someone else's task.

Speaking of which. The disappearance into the work. The artist sets up her easel in the gap of the unknown, but the poet has nothing to anchor herself and frequently falls in. Oh yes, I know, it's not always like that on either side. But you can't tell me, if you're a poet, you don't immediately relate to the rat gnaw.

So we're drawn to them. And one day a hundred years from now there will be a matching game, in one column a list of poets, and in the other a list of artists who were immortalized in verse. Half of the artists will have been forgotten, and over half of the poets will be forgotten. A couple of lines resembling telephone wires or clothes lines drawn from one column to the other but in a hundred years, no one will know what those are either.

NOTES

"It Must Have Been Weird" was read as a Keynote lecture at the launch of the CWRC (Canadian Writing Research Collaboratory) Project in September, 2011.

"Swoon" was published on Truck, an online magazine.

"Things that run through my head when writing an ekphrastic poem" was published on Lemon Hound.

"Oh How It Loves You," was published in Eleven Eleven.

The section titled, "Conventions of Ekphrasis" was inspired in part by a list posted on Lisa Rhody's website "Revising Ekphrasis."

In the poem "Poetry Is," I borrow the image of the tiger's lustre from D.H. Lawrence who said: "The living self has one purpose only; to come into its own fullness of being as a tree comes into full blossom, or a bird into spring beauty, or a tiger into lustre."

In "Video Art," the trail of ash might remind the reader of Leonard Cohen's words: "Poetry is just the evidence of life. If your life is burning well, poetry is just the ash."

ACKNOWLEDGEMENTS

Asking was written with the support of grants from the Alberta
Foundation of the Arts and the Edmonton Arts Council.

With thanks to Maureen Whyte and Robert Priest. Thank you to Rolf
Busch for the cover design.

Always grateful to friends in writing, especially those who read this in
progress: Nina Berkhout, Lee Elliott, Kimmy Beach, Barb Langhorst,
Annette Woudstra.

This book is for Rob and Chloe.